THE LOST PROVINCE

OR

THE WORTH OF BRITAIN

GREGYNOG LECTURES, 1948

THE LOST PROVINCE

OR

THE WORTH OF BRITAIN

BY

M. P. CHARLESWORTH

F.B.A., F.S.A., Hon. D.Litt. (Wales)

Fellow of St. John's College, Cambridge

CARDIFF
UNIVERSITY OF WALES PRESS
1949

PRINTED IN GREAT BRITAIN

PREFACE

THE purpose of these Lectures will (I hope) become clear in the reading of them: briefly, I have tried to set out why the Romans first conquered and afterwards remained in this island; then in what ways its occupation proved useful and profitable to them; finally, what they have bequeathed to us. On this last topic I have ventured to stress some less familiar methods of approach, and if sometimes I may appear dogmatic I hope later to have fuller opportunity of justifying them. I have retained the colloquial lecture form, and have not attempted to encumber a short text with lengthy notes, though I trust the references to sources and authorities will be sufficient to enable readers to check my views.

I would like here to express my warm thanks to Sir Ifor Williams, Professor Henry Lewis, and Mr. Thomas Jones for their friendship and ready help over matters concerning the Welsh language, and to my audience of March, 1948, at Aberystwyth, who gave me the greatest encouragement. Mrs. J. Bromwich, Professor W. B. Anderson, Mr. E. B. Birley, Professor Emrys Bowen, Mr. P. Hunter Blair, Mr. S. N. Miller, Dr. I. A. Richmond, Mr. C. E. Stevens, Mr. T. C. Lethbridge, and Mr. R. P. Wright have all spared precious time to supply me with information, and it is a pleasure to acknowledge my indebtedness to them. Several other friends, Professor F. E. Adcock, the Rev. W. O. Chadwick, Mrs. N. K. Chadwick,

Mr. Elwyn Davies, Mr. A. G. Lee, and Dr. I. A. Richmond, have been good enough to read the lectures (either in typescript or in proof) and I owe much to their corrections and suggestions, while a pupil of mine, Mr. R. M. H. Shepherd, of St. John's College, has spent time and work unstintingly on checking the references. My thanks are also due to Dr. V. E. Nash-Williams for his great kindness in putting at my disposal a block of the latest and most up-to-date map of Roman Wales to illustrate the text, and to Mr. G. W. Puttick for drawing the map of the Saxon Shore defences on both sides of the Channel with such skill and artistry. I should have liked to include a general map of Roman Britain, but felt that the size of the page would hardly allow it, and so would recommend readers to refer to the second edition of the admirable Ordnance Survey Map of Roman Britain.

Finally, I must express my warmest thanks for the delightful hospitality of Principal and Mrs. Ifor Evans during my stay in Aberystwyth, and also to Professor Emrys Bowen, Professor Davies, Dr. Thomas Jones, *C.H.*, Professor Treharne, Mr. Hugh Price and others who entertained me and made my stay so pleasant and memorable. I can only hope that this small book will not be entirely unworthy either of its subject or of the many kind friends who have helped me over its making.

M.P.C.

CONTENTS

THE YEARS OF CONQUEST

IT will probably best serve my purpose if I confess
at the outset why, when offered the honourable
office of Gregynog Lecturer for 1947–8, I chose
a subject which (for lack of a better term) I have
described as 'The Worth of Britain.' During those
uncertain years of 1939–45 the tasks of a civilian,
at once an academic and a clergyman, were
numerous and sometimes surprising: to teach and
lecture in Classics, to attend and sometimes preach
at special services, to fire-watch, to travel about the
country lecturing at schools, to address groups of
soldiers, to guide parties of guests over the college,
endeavouring the while to explain the apparent
illogicality of the English university and college
system—these were but a few of them. During
all that anxious time I found myself sustained not
only by these various contacts, but by re-reading
and reflecting upon the history of our country;
whatever the region, every place I visited provided
in an astonishing way some new aspect of our
history, some fresh reminder of its incomparable
richness and variety. That, in its turn, increased
an already deep interest in the study of Roman
Britain, as the one point where my own field of
work touched our history; this may explain why
I am now venturing to put before you some aspects
of Roman Britain, which seem to me of profound
and abiding value.

But first to some disclaimers.

My purpose is not to retell the history of Roman Britain, for that has been done many times, notably by such men as Haverfield and Collingwood, and for Wales itself by the revered Sir John Edward Lloyd. Nor is it to speak of the archaeology, for that has been done and is being done by many: in England by Dr. I. A. Richmond, and in Wales by Sir Cyril Fox and Dr. V. E. Nash-Williams. Rather, what I have asked myself is a question somewhat neglected so far—or rather a series of questions (which I am going to put to you)—'Why did the Romans choose to incorporate this distant island in their Empire? Why, that once done, did they retain it for nigh on four hundred years? What did they gain from the occupation? And what have we gained, or what did this island retain when the legions had departed?' To my mind these are questions that badly need asking, for we are so accustomed to the fact of Roman Britain, it has become so much a part of our national consciousness, that we are inclined to take the Roman conquest for granted, and to assume that it was perfectly natural that the Romans should come here. But it was not, and I feel that everyone who is interested in the history of our land ought to ask himself these questions and wish them answered. Or—to come down from these moral heights—let me confess to finding such questions fascinating, and ask you to allow me to suggest some answers. For the answers may illustrate the curious and paradoxical situation of Britain with regard to the Continent, and the alternations through which our History swings: we are part of Europe, yet on Europe's furthest fringes: our most famous river, 'sweet Thames', and some smaller ones open towards continental estuaries and invite approach;[1] yet others, including the Severn, flow westwards, facing towards Ireland and the vast ocean, and indicate a way of escape from invaders. At some moments, then, we look to the mainland to receive the vital currents of arts and civilization, at others we turn our back resolutely, shut ourselves off, and write our declaration of independence. It is a long story of attraction and repulsion, leading at some times to the flowering of a branch of literature or of art— I think of Chaucer—at others to a spirit of disapproval such as inspired that curiously-named pamphlet, *Edward the Confessor's Ghost* (wherein all our evils were attributed to conquest by the Normans),[2] or caused our great aunts to shake their heads over the goings-on of 'our naughty neighbours across the Channel.'

Yet I cannot embark straightaway upon the answers. Some preliminary historical outline is essential, so as to afford a framework, to emphasize certain facts or tendencies which need that emphasis, and also to give a glimpse of the latest investigations

---

[1] See Sir C. Fox, *The Personality of Britain*, ed. 4, 1943, 15.
[2] I owe my knowledge of this to Mr. H. Sykes Davies.

and of some achieved results.[1] Then, in the third
and fourth lectures, I hope to indicate what may
be answers to the questions I propounded earlier.

Perhaps I may begin most fittingly in 51 B.C.
and in northern France. All France lies at the
feet of the conqueror, Caesar: a few chieftains still
carry on a guerilla warfare, Commius amongst
them; then Commius surrenders, but in view of
his fear asks for one mercy, that he need never see
a Roman face again. That is what he said, though
I fancy that 'fear' meant 'hatred,' hatred of the
efficient power that had overrun his country and
deprived it of freedom; but his petition was
granted, and he came to Britain, there to found
a royal line. His story is representative of a
hundred others, at different times and ages, of men
and women broken and desperate, fleeing to this
island to preserve some fraction of liberty. Indeed,
when Caesar himself came here, the eastern part of
England was already full of such immigrants,
Belgae, crowded together, who had driven back
the earlier inhabitants to the interior.

Of Caesar's one serious invasion I need hardly
speak, beyond remarking the forces he brought—
five legions and some 2,000 cavalry, say rather
more than 25,000 men—and stressing the fact that
he imposed tribute; though the British could soon

[1] I must express here my gratitude to several friends, including Mr. Eric
Birley, Prof. Emrys Bowen, Mr. P. Hunter Blair, Mr. Thomas Jones,
Mr. S. N. Miller, Dr. I. A. Richmond, Mr. C. E. Stevens, and Mr. R. P.
Wright for allowing me to draw on their knowledge and patience, and for
advance notice of some of their publications.

forget to pay it, Italy did not forget that Britain had once been claimed as Roman territory. So we may understand why his successor, Augustus, never renounced the notion that Britain was to be occupied again one day, though he prudently managed to find excuses for not doing so himself.

First among his reasons for occupation was doubtless the reputed wealth of our island: corn, cattle and hides, slaves and hounds were some of its exports—and there were rumours of precious metals inland. But another reason was (I think) a curious geographical error, which begins in Caesar's time, and lasted—as errors do—long. Julius Caesar, in a cursory description of our island, declares it to be triangular in shape, and goes on to say that the second side (by which he means our western coast) faces towards Spain and the Western Sea, and on this quarter lies Hibernia. In fact, the geographical picture that most Romans had was of Spain with Cape Finisterre jutting out and up towards the north-west, and of Ireland lying between that cape and Britain. Even that great writer, Tacitus, shares this error; his father-in-law, Agricola, had (as he tells us) considered the conquest and occupation of Ireland as quite feasible, 'for Ireland, lying as it does midway between Britain and Spain and easily accessible from the Gaulish Sea, would have linked the strongest part of the Empire together' (he means Britain, Gaul, and Spain) 'with mutual advantages for all.' In this grandiose conception the four

5

lands would have been four sets of provinces, with one Atlantic lake enclosed between them. Though that great scientific geographer Ptolemy knew better, later ages did not. In the early fifth century Orosius declares firmly that Corunna faces towards Britain, and that Ireland, sited between Britain and Spain, looks from the mouth of the river Scena (Shannon?) distantly towards Spain. That particular geographical error lasted till at least the eleventh or twelfth century, as can be seen from the map of Henry of Mainz.[1]

Thus the Romans could produce one perfectly sound geographical reason for occupying Britain; it would help to link together the strongest provinces of the Empire. Secondly, an independent Celtic island was bound to be a refuge for malcontents, and an incentive to liberation movements: a free Britain must mean a rebellious Gaul. A third reason was that Rome never forgot that Julius Caesar had claimed Britain as Roman; his descendants would return one day. To these reasons circumstances after the year 40 added three motives: one, some discontented British leaders had fled to Gaul, to the protection of Rome, and Rome had refused to surrender them; so the Britons had been harassing the Gallic coast with raids. Secondly the reigning emperor Claudius longed for a brilliant feat of arms to inaugurate his accession to the throne, and to obliterate the memory of a ludicrous attempt by his predecessor, Caligula.

[1] See F. J. North in *Arch. Camb.* XC, 1935, 1.

Lastly, we must remember the disunity of Britain, the hostility felt by the older inhabitants towards the new fierce arrivals, the Belgic tribes. In Gaul lack of unity and tribal jealousies had worked powerfully for Julius Caesar: in Britain the older tribes—beaten, dispossessed, and pushed back— might actually welcome the Romans as deliverers.

So Claudius deliberately chose Britain for this exploit in 43. Both in the number of legions and in the route followed the plan of campaign adhered closely to Caesar's; five legions were selected— the II Augusta, the IX Hispana, the XIV Gemina, and the XX Valeria Victrix and the whole (or large part of) VIII.[1] This formidable array of legionaries, some 27,000 men, was accompanied by a large body of *auxilia* (native troops), and the total numbers probably fell little short of 50,000. Under the very able commander-in-chief, Aulus Plautius, who had brigadiers of solid merit to support him (e.g. the future Emperor Vespasian), victory over the chief tribe, the Trinovantes, was achieved by early autumn; Camulodunum (Colchester) was to be a Roman city and capital of the newly-acquired province, while the tribes who had made their submission on north and south (Iceni and Regnenses) were accepted as allies. During the next seven years advances proceeded with startling rapidity: in the west Exeter was reached, the lead-mines on the Mendips began to be

---

[1] See F. Oswald, in *Homenagem a Martins Sarmento*, 1933, 269, for the VIIIth legion.

exploited, and the IInd legion was settled at Gloucester; the XIVth and XXth proceeded across the midlands and by 50 may have reached Uriconium (Wroxeter) on the river Severn, while the IXth was settled at Lincoln. By 60 an ambitious governor was campaigning in North Wales and had even reached Anglesey,[1] when he was recalled by news of a terrible revolt in the east. But though that revolt was stamped out, the government decided on a policy of pacification and consolidation, in preference to premature advances. The damaged cities were rebuilt, and properly fortified; near Cambridge a short navigable canal,[2] connecting two river-systems, was opened up; gentler governors were appointed. After 70, however, a new emperor, Vespasian, was on the throne, and he ordered a new 'forward' policy; the northern headquarters was advanced to York, and the armies began to feel their way into Wales. Frontinus established the IInd legion at Isca Silurum (Caerleon), and some of his troops moving forward up the Usk valley planted forts at Usk, Abergavenny, and near Brecon (*Y Gaer*); next, from Wroxeter, troops following up the Severn established positions at Forden Gaer and Caersws (near Moat Lane junction), one of the great communications-centres of Wales. Though a road

---

[1] Tacitus, *Ann.* xiv. 29 ; and see Sir C. Fox, *A Find of the Early Iron Age* . . ., 1945, esp. 51.

[2] The Cambridgeshire Car Dyke ; see Grahame Clarke in *Antiq. Journ.* (forthcoming).

between Brecon and Caersws has not been definitely traced, some connection there must have been, and we may believe that by 77 or so the Usk and the Severn bounded Roman Wales.

Now there arrived a governor, Cn. Julius Agricola, who in seven years' tenure extended Roman control over an astonishingly wide area. One short late summer campaign in North Wales terrorized the Ordovices who had been causing trouble there, and Agricola now planned for the holding of Wales by a scheme based on a great quadrilateral of forts—at Chester, Caernarvon, Caermarthen and Caerleon. Each of these forts, observe, was easily accessible by sea, and, as the years passed, forced labour laid down the roads that were to link them.[1] While others were carrying out the scheme Agricola now turned north and achieved an amazing series of successes. By the end of the second year his army had reached the line Newcastle–Carlisle, and Agricola selected Corbridge (on the north Tyne) as his advanced base. Next year, in spite of a rainy summer, a rapid reconnaissance reached the Tay, and the fourth year was spent in steady consolidation of the territory overrun: once again roads and defence were based on a quadrilateral, roughly Edinburgh, Glasgow, Carlisle, Corbridge.[2] In his fifth year Agricola seems to have been in the region of Galloway; a road leaves the main western route

---

[1] For general complaints see Tacitus, *Agric.* 31.
[2] See especially I. A. Richmond's paper in *J.R.S.* xxxiv, 1944, 34.

Carlisle–Glasgow at Castledykes, passes by a camp on Loudoun Hill, and seems to be making for the port of Irvine, where the fleet would find convenient anchorage.[1] From Loudoun Hill on a clear day you can espy the blue hills of Antrim, and the arrival of a fugitive Irish princeling moved Agricola to declare that a small force (one legion with some *auxilia*) could easily subjugate Ireland. But whatever his plan may have been, he did not put it into execution, but instead turned north.

Here a peculiar problem confronts the historian. From Stirling a whole series of Roman camps has been discovered, stretching north-eastwards to near Stonehaven, and then turning as though to make for the Keith Gap and Huntly. Our literary sources will only allow of two men who could have penetrated so far, either Agricola now or Severus in 210, and at the moment my vote goes for Agricola. In his advance up Strathmore he guarded his left flank by a chain of camps that blocked and controlled the river exits from the Highlands—the Earn at Dalginross, the Almond at Fendoch, the Tay at Inchtuthil, and the Isla at Cardean; the Roman fleet would protect his right flank and secure his transport. In the seventh campaign he brought the Caledonians to battle in the neighbourhood of the Keith Gap—historians may care to compare the operations that resulted in the battle of Culloden Moor in 1746, where

[1] Richmond (loc. cit.) to which should now be added S. N. Miller, in *J.R.S.* xxxviii, 1948, 15.

the Duke of Cumberland confronted much the same problems as did Agricola—and Caledonian resistance was shattered. Agricola may even have reached Inverness, and he certainly bade a squadron of the Roman fleet circumnavigate Britain and prove it to be an island. In seven years he had doubled the size of the province of Britain, and had crushed all armed opposition. In some forty years the extreme limits of occupation had been triumphantly reached.

But now, about the year 84, Agricola was recalled. Perhaps he had been too successful; his campaigns must certainly have been costly, and the emperor needed legions for service elsewhere, and indeed, soon after recalled one, the XIVth, from our country. Plainly the work of consolidation could begin again—the planting of forts and the laying of roads to control and pacify the newly-conquered territory. Where the legions were now stationed we cannot be sure, though the IInd apparently stayed firmly at Caerleon, watching both Wales and the south-west. Chester and York may still have been occupied, but Inchtuthil seems to have been intended as the northern headquarters, and Newstead on the river Tweed was garrisoned until the close of the century. Indeed, as a result of Agricola's campaigns, in the words of Mr. S. N. Miller, 'southern Scotland was controlled by means of at least three patrolled roads.'[1] That is:

[1] See his article cited in the Bibliography.

1. From Corbridge to Newstead and the river Forth;

2. From Carlisle up Annandale and by upper Clydesdale to the Forth;

3. From Newstead westwards to Castledykes and so by Loudoun Hill to the mouth of the Water of Irvine.

Shortly after the year 100, however, comes a change, possibly connected with the fact that the Emperor Trajan was preparing for war against Dacia: the advanced garrisons withdrew in orderly fashion from Scotland. Then obscurity descends on affairs in Britain for nigh on twenty years, but during that period we know there was disaster. For after 112 the IXth Legion apparently vanishes from the scene: reinforcements were rushed across from Germany;[1] the whole situation was so grave that the Emperor Hadrian himself visited Britain in 122. He brought with him from Germany one of his most trusted generals, A. Platorius Nepos, and the VIth (Victrix) Legion, and made a thorough survey of the situation for himself.

Hadrian was a realist; an emperor with a comprehensive grasp of the needs and resources of the empire. In the East he had the courage to relinquish part of what his predecessor had occupied; similarly he decided here that the line of demarcation must run further south. Scotland was, for the moment, to be abandoned; as a frontier work

---

[1] E.g. the detachments led by T. Pontius Sabinus (Dessau, *ILS*. 2726).

Hadrian planned one of the most ambitious and structurally complete systems that Rome had yet seen—far more formidable for example than the earthworks and palisade or wall and ditch already constructed on the German frontier. The execution of this grandiose scheme Hadrian entrusted to Nepos, and though alterations were made during the actual building, the whole scheme must be ascribed to Hadrian and his military advisers. Roughly described it amounts to this:[1] a Roman masonry wall, standing some 20 ft. above ground, was to run from Newcastle-on-Tyne to Bowness-on-Solway.   In front the wall was protected by a deep ditch, while it was patrolled along its whole length by troops who were accommodated during their tour of duty in mile-castles.   Between each mile-castle were two turrets where men could shelter and also reach ground if necessary.   At various spots along (and sometimes astride) the wall were large forts holding the rest of the permanent garrison, with gates opening on the rugged country to the northward.   'The result was a barrier of immense strength,' writes Dr. I. A. Richmond,[2] 'endowed with a highly flexible defence, designed to roll up the enemy against the obstacle which he was attempting to cross.'   Behind this ran a deep and broad dyke, which would effectually control traffic or large-scale movement from the south, and

[1] This description is drawn from the 10th edition, as revised by Dr. Richmond, of Collingwood Bruce's *Handbook to the Roman Wall*.
[2] I. A. Richmond, *Roman Britain*, 1947, 16 ; for a fuller treatment see the same writer's 10th edition of the *Handbook to the Roman Wall*.

so protected this military zone from the rear.
Furthermore, to guard against raids from Galloway
by sea, the forts and the mile-castles (though not
the connecting wall) were continued south-west-
wards from Bowness following the Cumberland
coast for a rough fifty miles.[1]   Units of the fleet,
separate centuries, detachment from legions and
auxiliary troops, all worked at the construction of
this elaborate and formidable barrier, which even
to-day in its ruins remains one of the most majestic
abiding monuments of a past empire.

Behind this great work the task of pacification
could go on, though a generation or two must pass
before the country as far south as York and Preston,
the territory of the Brigantes, could be regarded as
friendly.   But, roughly speaking, a line drawn
south from Chester to Exeter on the Devon coast,
and again from Chester north-eastwards to York,
would represent the western and northern limits of
the civilian area.   What was happening within that
area and in Wales needs mention later, but it will
be best to finish with Roman Scotland first.   For
Hadrian's Wall was so successful that twenty years
later his successor, Antoninus Pius (138–61),
allowed the Governor Lollius Urbicus to erect
a still more northerly barrier from Forth to Clyde.
The distance was much less (roughly 37 as against
73 English miles).   The material, turf, was cheaper

[1] Orosius, vii. 17, 7, who ascribes the building of the wall to Septimius
Severus, remarks that it was 132 miles from sea to sea.   For the stretch
from Wallsend to Bowness this is an exaggeration, but if the west coast
forts are included, the figure is not so far out.

and easier to handle, and from the large new area brought under control more native troops could readily be enlisted. For some fifty years Hadrian's Wall was given up as a barrier; 'the doors were taken off the mile-castle gateways, and the rearward boundary dyke systematically breached.'[1]

To the immediate south of this Antonine Wall, that is in the Scottish Lowlands, came a network of main roads and of lateral roads, protected by forts and blockhouses. In England the country of the Brigantes, the northern counties, was checked and controlled in much the same fashion, as a glance at the Ordnance Survey Map of Roman Britain will show. The story of what was happening in Wales is uncertain, but amid the obscurity one or two facts seem to stand firm.[2] First, that while a great many forts were drained of their garrisons to supply strength for the northern defences, a few vital points were held firmly; the fine stone amphitheatre at Caerleon was temporarily disused after 120, though detachments certainly remained there; a Spanish cavalry regiment, the Vettones, left Brecon for Binchester; some forts, e.g. Coelbren, Penydarren, Gellygaer, were probably evacuated; but Caernarvon, Caersws, Brecon, and Caerleon were still garrisoned, albeit economically,[3] and Forden Gaer in its central position was heavily occupied in the last half of the

[1] I. A. Richmond, *Roman Britain*, 17.

[2] See generally R. E. Mortimer Wheeler, *Prehistoric and Roman Wales*, 1925, 230 ff.

[3] V. E. Nash-Williams, *The Roman Legionary Fortress at Caerleon*, 1940, 12–3.

second century.[1]   Rome neglected or left severely
alone the westward extensions of territory, e.g. the
Llŷn peninsula and Pembrokeshire; possibly a
little police-post at Castle Flemish (Amblestone)
was occupied early, but not beyond Hadrian's
time.[2] Otherwise it looks as though Rome was
experimenting with a policy of leaving the tribal
chieftains to rule and police their own tribesmen,
while she retained and manned certain essential and
nodal points. For the time being Wales gave
little trouble.

The second century, however peaceful in the
south, ended with a resounding disaster in the
north, mainly because an ambitious governor,
Clodius Albinus, decided to put in a claim for the
imperial throne, and in order to support himself
removed a great part of the British army to the
Continent.[3]   That gave an opportunity to the mal-
content tribes within (e.g. the Brigantes) and to
the enemies without, of showing what they felt,
and well they used it.   But before describing that
and the Roman recovery (as I try to do in my
second lecture) I would ask you to pause and
enquire what Rome had gained, after a century
and a half of occupation. If we scrutinize our
evidence impartially we must admit that down to
about A.D. 150 Rome, in keeping an army of about
40,000 men in garrison here, although she gained

---

[1] For reports on Forden Gaer, which in earlier publications is called Caer
Flos, see *Bull. Board Celt. Stud*. iii, 1925–7, 97, and iv, 1927–9, 277, and
also *Arch. Camb*. 1927, 333 ; 1929, 100 ; and 1930, 115.

[2] *Arch. Camb*. 1923, 211–22.

[3] Dio Cassius, lxxv, 4.

in some particulars, was footing a very heavy bill for benefits that are not immediately apparent to us. True, as we shall see, Britain was a reservoir of armed force that could supply help to and reinforce weak places, but apart from certain military and strategic advantages the full development of Britain's resources was still to come. Long-sighted emperors perhaps guessed or foresaw the utility of clinging to Britain, but the average educated man was less impressed. A Roman citizen from Egypt, who had risen to high judicial posts in the capital, by name Appian, about the year 150 compiled a history of Rome and of her wars, and in his *Preface* he makes reference to Britain. He is speaking of the various islands, great and small, which the Romans have occupied, and adds: 'they have even crossed the northern ocean to the Britannic island (which is larger than a large mainland) and hold the most important part of it, over half. They do not need the rest of it, for even the part which they do occupy is not profitable to them.'[1] It may possibly be that Appian here is apologizing for the withdrawal from those parts of Scotland north of the Antonine Wall, and for the fighting that continued in the lowlands, but he seems to represent current 'semi-official' opinion of the middle of the second century. Time alone would show whether it was right, or whether the occupation was really advantageous, and in the second lecture we must turn our attention to the troubled and exciting, but vital, third and fourth centuries.

[1] Appian, *Praef.* 5.

II

ROMANS AND BRITONS

THE second century in Roman Britain closed in disaster. How had that happened? The answer must be sought in the history of the empire at the time; civil war had broken out, and victory in that civil war had fallen, as so often, to the most ruthless of the competitors, Septimius Severus (A.D. 192–211). The last claimant he had to meet was a man who, as a soldier, bore a higher reputation than himself, Clodius Albinus, who at the time (192–7) was governor of Britain. Albinus, in order to fight with a fair chance of victory, relied on the British legions whom he ferried across the Channel, and in the final battle of Lyons, 197, they fought magnificently and worthily of their reputation[1]—but the island had been denuded of troops. The barbarians, seizing such an opportunity, broke through the gaps left in the defences, swarmed over an unprotected country and wreaked their hatred on all traces of the Romans: the evidence of burning, of deliberate smashing of large stones and slabs, of wanton destruction is clear. So Septimius must come out to punish, and to build up again; he made punitive raids on a vast scale against the Maeatae and the Caledonii; it is alleged that he reached the very north of Scotland. But he decided finally now where the future frontier must be, on a line that corresponds roughly to the present-day border between England and Scotland. The wall

[1] Herodian, iii. 7.

was repaired, fully and extensively, so extensively indeed that after-ages for long regarded Severus as the original builder, and the wall as his greatest achievement;[1] in front of the restored wall, advanced posts, stretching forward their *antennae* into hostile territory and garrisoned by scouts, could give early warning of movements from the north; such were High Rochester, Risingham, Bewcastle, and Netherby.

This was not his only task: the invaders in their fury had penetrated even farther south, wrecking and destroying; repair and reconstruction work was necessary at such fortresses as York and Chester in England. Even in Wales traces of rebuilding at Caernarvon, Caersws, Castell Collen and Caerleon, indicate how vigorous and how all-embracing Septimius' activity was. Wales was to be held, communications restored, the key-points adequately secured. This hard-headed ruler had decided that Britain was well worth keeping; he would never have expended this vast amount of energy, labour, and money upon a non-paying proposition. Claudius had deliberately chosen Britain for conquest, Septimius found it best fitted for large schemes of reconquest.[2] Not only were the enemy terrorized, and the defences of the country renewed and reinforced, but for greater ease in administration Septimius divided the British

[1] S.H.A. *Sev.* 18, 2 ; Orosius, vii. 17, 7 ; Bede, *H.E.* i. 5.
[2] Aurelius Victor, *de Caesaribus*, xx, *Sev.* 18, 'his maiora aggressus, Britanniam, quae ad ea utilis erat, pulsis hostibus, muro munivit.'

province into two, and henceforward our country
is referred to as 'the Britains.'

On the Continent, now, for some fifty years from
235 to 285, there followed a frightful period of
storm and stress, when Rome's enemies began to
batter at her defences on east and west and centre.
But our country, protected as ever by the sea,
enjoyed from about 160–270 her most prosperous
and peaceful period (apart from the great raid
before 200). The large landed estates, the *villae*,
were fully employed in farming *plus* rural industries; the country, with sturdy British ploughmen
and peasants to do the work was producing corn;
cattle and flocks were abundant; horses were being
bred in Lincolnshire.[1] With all these topics I hope
to deal more fully later, here I can merely mention
them. One strong proof of Britain's value to
Rome lies in the resolution with which the better
emperors clung to it. Nero alone, and he is
hardly a pattern of statesmanship, had contem-
plated surrendering it; sane and prudent rulers,
Vespasian, Hadrian, and Septimius, showed their
estimation of it by retaining it. In an hour of the
greatest peril—when, for example, the auxiliary

---

[1] This is not mere imagination. A British ploughman and his oxen are
represented in a splendid little statuette found at Piercebridge in Co. Durham
(*B.M. Guide to the Antiq. of Rom. Brit.* 1922, p. 90, or Rostovtseff, *Soc.
& Econ. Hist. Rom. Emp.*, pl. xxxi); the flocks of Britain and its wealth
generally are pictured on the Capheaton patera from Northumberland
(Rostovtseff, l.c. pl. xxxi, or *J.R.S.* xiii, 1923, p. 99); a fine tessellated pavement from Horkstow, Lincs., gives a vigorous representation of a chariot
race (Hinks, *B.M. Catalogue Gk. Etrusc. & Rom. paintings and mosaics*,
1933, fig. 124).

troops in Upper Germany had simply been annihilated,[1] when Gaul was in rebellion, and the East setting up pretenders—the great fighting Emperor Aurelian (270–275), decided to abandon the province of Dacia and draw the frontier at the Danube. But he did *not* abandon Britain. If we ask why, there can only be one answer: because Aurelian thought it of value.

But about 275 Britain began at long last to experience what trouble could be. A migratory Irish tribe, the Dessi, began raiding south-western Wales, and the *villae* there show marks of it: about the year 300 sudden disaster overtook one such estate at Llantwit Major; forty-one human skeletons and the bones of three horses are mute but grim evidence of the calamity, and though life there staggered on for another half-century, it was weakened and broken. Yet another *villa*, at Ely near Cardiff, surrounded with earthworks, met its end about 325. A fortified building at Cwmbrwyn, near St. Clears, the continued repair work on the roads leading westward, the coin-hoards found round about Fishguard and farther inland— all these are evidence for the trouble and panic caused by the Irish raiders.[2] Thus, the danger was no longer from the north—Severus had done his work well enough—but from Irish raiders on

[1] See H. Nesselhauf, *Die spätrömische Verwaltung der gallischgermanischen Länder.* Abhand. Preuss. Akad. 1938, Ph.-Hist. Klasse, No. 2, 47.

[2] For Cwmbrwyn see *Arch. Camb.*, 1907, 175; there are four milestones of the late third century between Cardiff and Neath, *plus* two in Carmarthenshire; see R. E. Mortimer Wheeler, *Roman and Native in Wales*, App. iii, esp. 93–4.

21

the south-west and Saxon raiders on the south-east.
This change in the angle of approach is reflected by
a move of the Legio II Augusta. After a stay of
nearly 200 years at Caerleon the authorities
apparently shifted the bulk of the legion to Richborough—where it was conveniently near for
transshipment across the Channel; of the remainder
some, perhaps, were transferred to a new fort at
Cardiff, while others must have been left to
garrison Caerleon itself. Against the sea-raiding
Saxons some governor or ruler (perhaps Carausius
initiated the scheme, Constantius almost certainly
completed it) carried through an elaborate defence-
scheme of forts along the coast (with naval squadrons based on them) that watched for the approach
of raiders and could despatch forces to meet them,
either on sea or by land; this line of forts stretched
from the Wash to the Isle of Wight—Saxon Shore
forts. (See further pp. 47–48.) But though the
coasts might be harried, Britain inland was comparatively undisturbed, and Constantius (293–306)
was actually able to despatch masons and craftsmen
from our island to repair and restore ruined towns
in France, such as Autun. Meanwhile, he himself carried out a complete and profound rebuilding
of the defence scheme in the north. 'Evidence has
steadily accumulated,'[1] writes Dr. Richmond, 'to
show that Constantius was not satisfied with patch-
work. His was a new creation, planned and
executed in the light of new ideas; and where

[1] *Arch. Ael.*[4] xiii. 1936, 182.

foundations were not firm, his work was as drastic
as Hadrian's in days long past.' The impressive
multangular tower at York or the massive new
fortifications of High Rochester are still visible
proofs of that activity. When he died at York on
July 25th, 306, his soldiers were persuaded to
acclaim his son Constantine as successor to the
imperial purple, the first time (but not the last)
that the fiery and independent army of Britain
raised a man to the throne. Six years later
Constantine set out from Britain upon his great
adventure to win Rome for himself, and that
audacious exploit was never forgotten by the poets
and story-tellers of later Celtic ages, nor indeed by
the next two or three generations.

But Constantine when he departed did not
empty Britain of forces. Raids there were still
and attacks, but so successful for fifty years and
more was the defence-system—the wall, the armies,
the Saxon Shore forts and flotillas—that then something utterly new happened: the barbarians care-
fully combined together in a planned assault.
What Augustus and early emperors had dreaded
—simultaneous attacks from several quarters—now
came true: Irish raiders, Picts from the north, and
seaborne Saxons, joined together in 367 in a vast
barbarian agreement, a 'barbarica conspiratio'
(Ammian, xxvii. 8). The results were appalling:
the general in charge, the *Dux Britanniarum*, was
entrapped and killed, the commander of the Saxon
Shore fell in battle, the whole country was overrun

as far south as London. A full tide of invasion and ruin swept over the province; the slave-labour on which the *villae* partly depended escaped never to return; landowners and farmers were impoverished, or ruined, and flocked to the comparative security of the walled towns; hoards of buried silver-plate and coins attest the fear and flight of those terrible years. It is not surprising that, though the great general Theodosius restored the situation, the *villae* ceased to produce, and commerce dwindled. Nor is it surprising that, though Christianity was rapidly becoming the official religion, depression and continuing raids resulted in a swing of feeling back towards the old gods: in the last thirty years of the closing fourth century the pagan temple at St. Albans was remodelled, new temples arose in the enclosure of Maiden Castle and at Lydney, while at Cirencester (where there may have been a community of Christians) a governor proclaims that he had set up again a statue and a column 'of the old religion' that had apparently been thrown down by zealots.[1]

Not all parts of the country had been equally affected; for example, the district round Langton, in East Yorkshire, carried on apparently undisturbed in a quiet prosperity. But the blow of 367 had been mortal, and even Theodosius could not attempt a restoration of the same energy and completeness as Severus or Constantius. True,

---

[1] See F. Haverfield, *Archaeologia*, lxix, 1917, 161 ; see also p. 77 and note 2.

the wall and its forts were repaired, but *not* the
advanced posts of High Rochester or Bewcastle or
Netherby. Theodosius did, however, initiate a
new defence system for the East Coast, the signal-
stations of Yorkshire, extending probably from the
Humber up to the Tyne (see pp. 49–50). These
stations could observe the approach of raiders and
signal the news to the forces stationed inland, and
so give them time to counter any landing.

In 378 disaster overwhelmed the Roman Empire
at Adrianople; the only real hope henceforward of
manning Rome's depleted armies lay in foreign
and barbarian aid. The emperors showed a painful
interest in any means that might help to improve
military science and add to its resources. A
student of military art, Flavius Renatus Vegetius,
addressed a small pamphlet to the court about
older methods of selecting, drilling, and training
recruits, and received the gracious command of
imperial majesty to write more; so we possess the
four books *de re militari* of Vegetius, which are of
absorbing interest still for those who desire a
picture of how the Roman army was trained and
equipped, what were its artillery, its surveying and
its mining. A very different writer, an amateur,
recommended in a short treatise various impractic-
able measures, and put forward some strange
inventions of his own—e.g. a kind of paddle-boat
worked by oxen, and a sort of bladder-bridge
inflated by bellows—which somehow got filed
away among the papers of the Roman War Office.

25

c

But the situation was not to be met by crank devices: it was desperate; for ambitious governors or commanders were ready enough to make a bid for the throne, and one of them has left a name of imperishable glory in Celtic legend.

Magnus Maximus was a Spaniard by origin,[1] and may have been stationed in Britain from 375 onwards; possibly a governor, possibly a legionary commander, he was certainly dissatisfied by what he regarded as lack of recognition from Theodosius; in the spring of 383 his troops, disgusted with the ineffectiveness of the western emperor, Gratian, acclaimed Magnus as emperor and crossed with him to Gaul. For a time he was brilliantly successful: he overthrew Gratian, and zealously supported orthodoxy by persecuting the Priscillianist heretics in Spain, but in August, 388, he was trapped and killed at Aquileia.[2] But though Maximus left troops both to guard the Yorkshire signal-stations and to man the Saxon Shore forts, he removed Roman soldiers from the wall, for no Roman coins found on the wall can be dated later than 383. It might have been expected that the same fatal consequences would follow as in 197. But they did not, and to explain why, we must linger a little on this famous name.

Rome had by now brought into use the device of employing barbarian allied contingents, *foederati*, that is, troops bound by treaty to protect

[1] Zosimus, iv. 35, 3.
[2] Orosius, vii. 34, 9 ; Sulp. Severus, *Chron.* ii. 49 and 50, and *Vita S. Martini*, 20.

sections of her frontiers: barbarians, under their own king or chieftain, and fighting in their own formations, could now be settled on Roman territory upon conditions of defending it for Rome. Gratian had already had recourse to Franks as *foederati* in northern Gaul, and these Franks were apparently set to guard the line from Bavay to Tongres. Now I believe that Maximus adopted a similar measure; as a good soldier he could not leave the northern frontier defenceless, and it looks as though he entrusted this task to two northern allied peoples as *foederati* under their own kings, the Votadini in the east and the Damnonii on the west.

It is well known that at some period a king of these northern Votadini, Cunedda, settled in North Wales, and became the ancestor of several Welsh royal families, but at what period precisely has been hotly argued. On this point, I believe that Mr. Hunter Blair has made an important contribution, and that the date of Cunedda's migration must be assigned to about the year 450.[1] About that same year there was reigning a king of the region that was later to be called Strathclyde, Coroticus (Ceretic), who drew upon himself the censure of St. Patrick. Now among the immediate ancestors of both Cunedda and Ceretic are men with Latin names: Cunedda's father and grandfather were called Aetern (*Aeternus*) and Patern

---

[1] See P. Hunter Blair, in *Arch. Ael.* **xxv**, 1947, 1.

(*Paternus*); Ceretic's grandfather and great-grand-father were Cinhil (*Quintilius*) and Cluim (*Clemens*) respectively.   For about a century these two tribes, Votadini and Damnonii, living north of the wall, had been in free and friendly intercourse with the Romans, had intermarried with them and received something of their culture. Furthermore, Patern (Cunedda's grandfather) bears the title *Peisrut*, 'the man of the red tunic.' I would suggest to you, therefore, that Magnus Maximus, before leaving Britain, provided for its defence by making treaty-arrangements with these two northern people Votadini and Damnonii, and that he bestowed upon King Patern of the Votadini the insignia of a Roman military officer, which included a scarlet tunic. The Roman government had done its bene-ficent work; from enemies these two tribes had become friends, and from friends allies (*foederati*). Henceforth, in the north, British tribes, trained in Roman ways of fighting and in the use of Roman weapons,[1] were quite capable of defending their own country.

More follows: legend connects Magnus Maximus strongly with Wales and the Welsh garrison towns —Carmarthen (with Cadair Vaxen not far away), Caerleon, and Caernarvon (Caer Segeint).[2] When Maximus crossed the Channel on his attempt he must have taken with him troops from the western

[1] The phrase in *Gildas*, 18, 'exemplaria instituendorum armorum,' must imply something of the sort.

[2] Note that Nennius, 25, says there was an inscribed tomb of Constantine (Maximus' son) at Caer-Segeint.

and northern forts, and an unexpected confirmation of this fact has been won from the study of a late-Roman document (based on official sources) called the *Notitia Dignitatum*. This document mentions among troops garrisoning places in the Balkans a regiment called Seguntienses; these can only be a regiment from Seguntium, in fact from the fort at Caernarvon. How astonishing, but how pleasing, to find the *Notitia Dignitatum* and the *Mabinogion* combining together.[1]

For Maximus must have done something considerable and striking, something which made an enduring emotional impression on the minds of the Britons, to be enshrined as he is in legend and tradition. In Welsh memory he survives as Maxen Wledig (*Guletic*), a great ruler, the ancestor of several lines of Welsh kings. A Cornish miracle-play remembers him as Mytern Massen, 'Maximus the King.' He had married a bride from this island, Elen 'of the hosts,' a king's daughter at the least, a goddess at the most. Among his children, including Constantine and Pascentius,[2] was a daughter Sevira, who married Vortigern, the high king. Gradually Maximus comes to be thought of as a British hero, who had set out from this country, and conquered Rome—'Maximus, who killed the king of the Romans,' as King Concenn records it on the Eliseg pillar. Later, much later, he is the

---

[1] C. E. Stevens, in *Etudes Celtiques*, iii, Juin, 1938, 86.
[2] Note that the name Pascentia occurs on some of the christening spoons from the Mildenhall Treasure.

mighty emperor at Rome; he dreamed a dream that in the long run brought him journeying over many lands and seas to Caernarvon to claim his bride there and make her empress by his side. No people will thus take a ruler to its heart unless he has done some great and memorable thing for it, and my explanation is that Maximus the governor first recognized the two tribes in North Britain as allies, first gave a chieftain Roman insignia, and first entered into a marriage-alliance with a British royal line. If you like it—the history of an organized Welsh people begins with an act of recognition by this Spanish-born governor, Magnus Maximus.

Friendly relations had gone on for some time. Within a few years of Maximus' death a young Briton called Sucat was born of respectable Romano-British parents. St. Patrick, for that is the name Sucat subsequently bore (and I wish someone would explain when and why he was given the name of Patricius) declares that his father was a town-councillor and also a deacon, and that his name was Calpurnius; an Irish writer, Muirchu, records that his mother's name was Concessa, to which we may add that one British tradition records that he was born in territory formerly occupied by the Brigantes. Now though several regions contend for the honour of St. Patrick's birthplace, the two likeliest in my opinion are North Cumberland (or, rather, the country on both sides of the Solway) and South-East Wales.

A dedication from the Wall region, probably not later than the middle of the third century, reveals a local commander commemorating a victory over raiders and giving thanks for divine help; his name was Q. Calpurnius Concessinius.[1] It is at the least curious that he should combine both the family names of St. Patrick; similarly, one or two of the late Latin tombstones over the border display names—e.g. Carantius and Cupitianus—which were certainly borne by Roman soldiers and officers serving in the Wall region. Though slight, this evidence does in my view offer confirmation that Romans and Britons were intermarrying in this region, and explains how St. Patrick could regard his fellow-countrymen as at once citizens of Rome and members of that Damnonian kingdom over which Coroticus ruled.[2]

These new native allied defenders brought in by Maximus did their work well in the north, whereas the east and the south-west could not withstand consistent and increasing pressure. The Irish continued their raids on South Wales, and about 390 the Saxons overran and destroyed, after desperate fighting, the Yorkshire signal-stations which had for so long foiled them. Even so, Rome could still send reinforcements and a general, the famous Stilicho; he arrived in 395, and by punitive expeditions against the raiders and by reorganization of the whole northern defence-system, did what he could to safeguard the province.

[1] *CIL.* vii. 481.   [2] St. Patrick, *Epistula*, 2.

His reorganization involved the recognition that the Scottish lowlands, with the Wall region and Cumberland, were to be permanently under the control of the *foederati* kings, who would be responsible for their defence. Stilicho's new line was apparently based upon York, which retained its position as headquarters; the actual frontier perhaps ran from South Shields diagonally across County Durham to Bowes (and perhaps Brough) and so to Lancaster. To the north was federate territory, which would serve as a buffer, and troops could be despatched quickly to any threatened point by using the roads that radiated from York; Brougham was perhaps still occupied as an advance post, while Brough (at the northern end of the Bowes Moor Pass) and Catterick, remained important centres in this scheme. The forts were manned by regiments recruited locally, the Petuerenses, the Longovicani, etc. (*Not. Dign. Occ.* 40), while the hard core of the fighting troops was garrisoned at York. Even though raiders or armies penetrated the outer screen of the federate kingdoms, they would still have to reckon with strong forces defending the fertile plain of York and the lands to the south. In the eastern and southern regions Stilicho probably restored and repaired the Saxon Shore forts,[1] and then with the new defensive scheme for Britain completed returned to shoulder fresh tasks, to be celebrated in verse by the poet

[1] A tile at Pevensey bears the name of the Emperor Honorius on it; *Eph. Ep.* ix. 1281.

Claudian, and (eventually) to be murdered by the cowardly master he had so often saved.

By now, that is about A.D. 400, the Western Empire was beginning to disintegrate. The raids continued: in one such raid about 405–6 the Irish reached a farmstead belonging to Patrick's father,[1] killed some servants, and carried off Patrick and others, with sheep and cattle, to Antrim, where for six years he served as a slave. But these were petty local troubles compared with the sheer disaster that overwhelmed Roman western defences on the Continent; on December 31st of the year 406 a horde of barbarians (Alani, Suebi, Vandali) crossed the frozen Rhine in overwhelming strength, annihilated the frontier troops, captured Trier and poured into France and even as far as Spain; the Rhine was no longer a boundary; only in the far south, in Provence, did Roman territory remain comparatively undamaged. Amid this confusion and disorder, the British army chose for itself a new commander, by name Marcus. As in a short time he proved unpopular, the soldiers killed him and elected another, Gratian; in four months' time they again killed their choice, and acclaimed a ranking soldier with the well-omened name of Constantine. To kill their emperor was tending to become a habit with the soldiers, and Constantine prudently decided to give them something else to think about; he would cross over into France and try his fortune.

[1] The farm *may* have been near Bewcastle in Northern Cumberland ; see G. H. Wheeler in *E.H.R.* l, 1935, 109.

Repairs were carried out on the Yorkshire signal-stations;[1] two of his commanders, Justinian and Nebiogast, were sent on in advance across the Channel; finally he and his chief general, Gerontius, after due preparations, crossed with all available forces to the Rhine mouth.[2] Some success he had; he temporarily restored the Rhine defences, he was even recognized for a time as consul (in 409) and legitimate ruler by Honorius, but in 411 he fell in battle.

The year before, an event had occurred that must have sounded like the end of the world; in August, 410, Rome was sacked by the Goths. True, Rome was no longer a capital, no longer an administrative centre, but she had seemed something eternal and immovable; and now the barbarians had entered and ravaged. What happened in Britain we do not know precisely, but one ancient author speaks definitely of a revolt in which the British took up arms and freed their cities from the barbarians who threatened them; in that same year, 410, the Emperor Honorius informed 'the cities' in Britain that they must 'look after themselves' (Zosimus, vi. 5, 3, and 10, 2). The situation, to my mind, is that Constantine had removed all Roman troops from Britain in order to back his attempt; Honorius' message need

---

[1] This seems a possible date for the late inscription at Ravenscar recording some repair work ; *J.R.S.* ii, 1912, 210.

[2] Zosimus, vi. 2. Mrs. Bromwich points out to me the remarkable fact that Constantine and Gerontius (*Geraint*) are regular names for Cornish kings.

mean no more than that he could not *at the moment* spare any troops for Britain. By encouraging the British cities, the only centres where responsible administrative officials remained, to look after themselves I think he still hoped for a re-occupation when the storm had been weathered. Certainly we gather from the same historian (ibid. vi. 5, 3) that the Britons rescued themselves from their enemies, and it is worth noting that when St. Patrick, after years of absence, revisited his home and kindred, he found them safe and well, and anxious only that he should not leave them again; the date of that visit cannot be much later than 415.[1]

After this year events are but dimly discerned, and the scanty evidence is differently interpreted by different scholars; I can only present here what seems to me a rough probable outline. Honorius had not abandoned the island; Roman civil officials were still there; in view of the state of the Empire he could not send reinforcements—that was all. But eight years after his despatch I think some definite action was taken. In 418 Honorius ordered the *Praefectus Praetorio* of Gaul to summon a council (of the Seven Provinces) to meet at Arles,[2] which had succeeded Trier as the administrative capital for Gaul. Now the Anglo-Saxon chronicle under this year 418 has an

---

[1] St. Patrick, *Confessio*, 23, and Bury, *Life of St. Patrick*, 41.
[2] See D. G. Haenel, *Corpus Legum ab imp. Rom. ante Justinianum lat.*, Leipzig, 1857, 238, No. 1171 ; cf. E. Stein, *Gesch. d. Spätrömischen Reiches* i, 1928, 409–10.

35

interesting entry: we read that 'in this year the Romans collected all the treasures that were in Britain, and hid some in the earth so that no man might afterwards find them, and conveyed some with them into Gaul.' This does, I believe, mark a real evacuation, when government officials with their records and their treasures were recalled into France, and it may well be that one result of the Council of Arles was the momentous decision to evacuate Britain completely.[1]

Possibly now in the north and west the famous British chieftain, Vortigern, was at the head of a rebel and anti-Roman party, determined to throw off the Roman yoke and to live in their own way (Zosimus, vi. 5, 2), while in the south-east and east the population still thought of itself as Roman (St. Patrick did) and retained Roman titles for its magistrates and officials. Possibly, too, the rebels had embraced the British heresy of Pelagianism just because it was *not* the official Roman religion; this may explain why St. Germanus arrived in this island in 429, and according to tradition not only refuted the heretics with his heavenly eloquence, but also deposed a native king. For St. Germanus was no ordinary bishop; a Roman, trained in law and rhetoric, he had been governor of a province before he was elected Bishop of Auxerre,[2] and

---

[1] After this date there begins the gradual flight of Britons over into Armorica, which is later called 'lesser Britain,' that is Brittany ; cf. J. Loth, *L'Emigration bretonne* . . . 1883.

[2] See W. Levison's introduction to Constantius' Life of St. Germanus in *Mon. Germ. Hist.* (Script. rerum Meroving.) vii, 1920, edd. B. Krusch and W. Levison, 225–30.

was a person of exceptional weight and authority. Doubtless the Roman government in Gaul was prepared to send agents if it could not send armies, and the church would certainly co-operate. In the south of England, at any rate, there were still men with Roman titles prepared to obey Rome's instructions, for St. Germanus healed the son of a man 'tribuniciae potestatis,'[1] and we may mark how the names TRIBUNUS (or TRIFUN) and PROTICTOR occur on some late tombstones and in genealogies. Yet equally certainly there were no official Roman commanders, for the population begged St. Germanus (who had seen service in his younger days) to lead their levies into battle against the combined forces of Picts and Saxons; the result was the 'Alleluia Victory' and the crushing rout of the invaders.

Difficulties there are in this account,[2] yet in substance it looks very like an attempt to reassert Roman authority, to hearten and encourage the pro-Roman element that still stood steadfast in the country. Something of a kindred purpose may be discerned three years later, for in 432 St. Patrick, now consecrated as Bishop for Ireland, set out on his great mission to organize and strengthen the existing Christian communities there, and to preach to and convert others; conquest was no

---

[1] Constantius, *Vita S. Germani* (ed. Levison), 15.

[2] For instance, in the traditional siting of the victory near Mold in Flintshire, which seems an unlikely place for a combination of Picts and Saxons. We may note that Selby Abbey had some association with the saint, and the Humber region would provide a more likely site.

longer even thinkable, but to win these barbarians
for orthodox Christianity was in some degree to
Romanize and civilize them. Tradition has it
that Germanus came a second time to Britain, and
we know that in or after 446 the Britons made a
last despairing appeal for help to the great Roman
general commanding in Gaul, Aetius[1]—though we
do not know the answer to that appeal. Now the
latest date for Germanus' second voyage appears to
be 447 (the limits lie between 435 and 447[2],) and
I like to think that in that year St. Germanus
gave one order of lasting importance. On his
previous visit he had, by his authority and holiness,
ejected an unworthy British king from office; on
this occasion—is it not possible?—he carried an
order or an instruction to Cunedda, the reigning
king of the Votadini, to protect British territory
against Irish raiders (and even settlers) by moving
his family and his tribesmen down into North
Wales. If so—and I say *if* with emphasis, for no
one realizes more keenly than I that we are moving
in a cloud of hypotheses—*if* so, it was a decisive
action for the history of this island and of Wales,
just as it was certainly the last expression of
Roman will in this country.

For after the middle of the fifth century Britain
is a lost province of the Empire; western Rome
could do nothing, and eastern Rome only knew
what Procopius wrote for them that 'Brittia is an

[1] Gildas, 20.
[2] See W. Levison (op. cit.).

island known by hearsay, containing a wall; east of that wall is a salubrious climate, and plenty reigns; to the west of it no one can live because of poisonous snakes and other terrors.'[1]   Yet these Romanized Britons, though the west could do nothing for them, and the east had forgotten them, put up a splendid resistance.   Think of the generations it took before Angles, Saxons, and Jutes had thoroughly occupied England alone; Wales they never conquered.   Then compare that with the forty years (say 43–83) in which the Roman forces overran and occupied all England and Wales (save Cornwall), right up to a line linking Carlisle and Newcastle.   Yet we may note that though Rome by her vast organizational power could make a speedy conquest of an enemy who was much less organized, her conquest has not remained; in the course of two centuries these slow but tenacious Anglo-Saxons gained the land in which they were finally to dwell, and both Celts and Saxons learned whether in fighting or in friendly intercourse to respect each other and eventually to become a united nation.[2]

With the year 450 we have reached the end of

---

[1] Procopius, *Bell. Goth.* iv. 20 (=viii. 20, 42–58).

[2] The fact of prolonged intercourse is shown by the way in which the British names of rivers, especially in the North and in the west Midlands, have survived.   So, too, names of forests : e.g. Kesteven, Barroc, Andred, Penge ; Lyme, Arden, Cannock, Morfe, Kinver, Kemble, Savernake, and Mendip.   See Sir F. M. Stenton's article (in the Bibliography).   Just as in English —*chester* or —*cester* suggests a Roman camp or settlement, so in Welsh—*Caer* or —*car* does.

our brief historical survey, for after that date, if not before, Roman authority was dead in Britain. My chief task remains before me, to attempt (with this historical framework in our minds) to make a sober estimate, first of Rome's gain, and then of our gain, from nigh on four hundred years' occupation of this our country.

III

WHAT ROME GAINED FROM BRITAIN

THE brief and summary historical survey contained in the last two lectures will have shown that not only did Rome occupy Britain for nearly four hundred years, but that she held on to it determinedly even though she sacrificed other advanced territories (e.g. Dacia), and made no attempt to recover land beyond the Rhine that was lost in the confusion and warfare of the third century. We must, therefore, ask ourselves why Rome should have clung so resolutely to a distant northern island, and what were the advantages that appealed to this eminently practical people.

At first, doubtless, a combination of strategic and political reasons swayed them. Independent Celtic kingdoms across the Channel might inflame conquered Gaul, and might aid insurgent movements by sending assistance or harass peace by raids, such as disturbed the Gallic coasts round about 40. In addition, hazy geographical notions may have fostered the opinion that an occupation of Britain, followed by that of Ireland, would link up with Spain, and so make 'an Atlantic lake' controlled by Rome. These motives were always present, and in addition, Claudius had personal reasons for wishing for a grandiose venture (with success guaranteed) to mark the opening of his reign. So came the invasion of 43, and ten years

D

saw notable advances; even so, Nero did contemplate for a moment abandoning the new province.[1] But the occupation of the lowland zone was rapidly completed, and the comparatively mild climate of our country[2] allowed Roman arms to penetrate farther north than on the Continent. 'Colder than a Gallic winter' was a Roman proverb, but in our island a large part of Scotland was held for two longish periods (80—c. 105 and from c. 140 to c. 190), and the Roman Wall zone in England lies far to the north of any region on the Continent occupied by the legions.

Prestige was doubtless, at first, a motive both for staying and for enlarging the area of occupation, but very soon the strategic importance of occupation began to reveal itself. It might be argued that a strong fleet, a *classis Gallica*, patrolling the north coast of France from the mouth of the Rhine to Brest, would have been equally effective and less expensive. But I doubt it, and in addition, the Romans were never 'fleet-minded.' But they knew well the value of manpower, and slowly began to realize that Britain was at once a source of manpower (in recruits for the armed forces), and also what I may call a defence-reserve.

Rome early began recruiting auxiliary regiments from the island population. Before the Flavian era, from the territory south of Mersey and Humber, there is evidence for the existence of one

[1] Suetonius, *Nero*, 18.
[2] Tacitus, *Agric.* 12.

cavalry squadron (*ala*), three *cohortes Britannorum*, and six *cohortes Brittonum*, making a total of nine infantry auxiliary regiments, or about 4,500 men. Later on, Flavian commanders added another three cohorts, and Nerva two more (each of 1,000 men); subsequent emperors recruited another five, most of which were milliary.[1] Thus, something like eighteen regiments, six of them milliary, were raised from the inhabitants of this country, making a grand total of 12,000 men, a very respectable figure, even when compared with the contributions of other provinces. Later on, after 140, when Lollius Urbicus occupied the lowlands of Scotland, we find evidence of several *numeri Brittonum* (units composed of native Britons) serving in Roman Germany. They were engaged in building and garrisoning the frontier forts in the Odenwald.[2] Nearly a hundred years later, in 232, inscriptions show us British native regiments repairing camp buildings at Walldürn near Miltenberg on the river Main.[3]   But it must also be remembered that as time went on native Britons could enlist and serve not only in auxiliary regiments from different countries, but also (by the end of the second century) even occasionally in legions. A tombstone on the Scottish Wall gives us the name and story of a native Briton: he was Nectovelius; a

---

[1] The figures in Cheesman (see bibliography) can now be corrected and improved : I owe my information to Mr. E. B. Birley, who kindly sent me his own list.

[2] Dessau, *ILS.* 2624 ; Mommsen, *Ges. Schrift.* vi. 166.

[3] Dessau, *ILS.* 9184.

Brigantian by birth, for nine years he had served as a soldier in the IInd Cohort of Thracians, and at the age of thirty he died (presumably in battle).[1] From the other end of the kingdom, at Colchester, comes a dedication by a Caledonian, named Lossio Veda, proud of his birth and ancestry, but ready to make an offering for the victory of the emperor: Caledonians were not at that time (c. A.D. 235) members of the Empire, but Veda had perhaps served in a cavalry *ala*, and may also have been connected with trooping between Colchester and the Rhine.[2] Any native lad, of adventurous or roving disposition, could easily find a place and a career in Roman forces, and Rome certainly drew largely on British recruits.

Secondly, Britain could be used as a strategic reserve. The very large forces collected for the invasion, five legions and a corresponding number of auxiliary troops—say 50,000 in all—were slightly reduced by about the year 50 to a permanent garrison of four legions and of auxiliaries. So, in the troublesome Civil War of 69 a governor of Germany obtained 8,000 legionaries from Britain[3] to reinforce the depleted legions, and a year later Vespasian sent for a crack formation from Britain, the Leg. XIV (*Gemina Martia Victrix*) to help put down a Batavian rebellion.[4] Shortly

---

[1] *CIL.* vii. 1091.

[2] Dessau, *ILS.* 4576 ; cf. F. Haverfield, in *Arch. Journ.* xlix, 1892, 188–9, and I. A. Richmond, in the same journal, ciii, 1946, 63–4.

[3] Tacitus, *Hist.* ii. 57.

[4] Tacitus, *Hist.* iv. 68.

after Agricola's conquest of the north Domitian removed one legion, and so reduced the permanent garrison to three; it was a reasonable (though slightly premature) step to take, considering that our island could now be regarded as thoroughly conquered, and that barbarian threats were visible in the regions of the middle and lower Danube.[1] Possibly the emperors drew a little too generously on Britain's reserves, for towards the end of Trajan's reign a revolt in north Britain caused damage, and called for Hadrian's own presence, which resulted in the famous Wall of Hadrian. Then followed an era of comparative stability, when no more drafts were made; indeed, Marcus Aurelius about 175 actually reinforced the troops of the garrison by sending here 5,500 heavy-armed Sarmatian horse-men,[2] who were irresistible in a charge and superbly useful in pursuing a beaten enemy. About the middle of the third century detachments from the British legions were stationed near Mitrovica (Sirmium) and helping the task of defence there (Dessau, *ILS*. 546), and possibly about the same period a warrant officer of the VIth Legion, L. Artorius Castus, led an expeditionary force (composed of detachments from the legions and auxiliary troops) against the Armoricani, that is the inhabitants of the region which is now Brittany, to quell a revolt there (Dessau, *ILS*. 2770).

---

[1] Detachments from all four legions had been despatched even before this date : Dessau, *ILS*. 9200.

[2] Dio Cassius lxxi. 16, 2, and see I. A. Richmond's remarks in *J.R.S.* xxxv, 1945, 15.

Lastly, we should notice how the needs of the later third century were met by the transfer, about 275, of a considerable section of the Legio II Augusta from Caerleon to Richborough: here they could not only take their share in the Saxon Shore defences, but at need could be ferried quickly across to the mouth of the Rhine if affairs in Germany called for it.[1] One grave weakness in the imperial scheme of defence was lack of reserves; the concentration of greater strength at one point nearly always involved weakening elsewhere. But Britain, quite apart from its usefulness as a recruiting area and as a training ground, was sufficiently strongly garrisoned to allow of the despatch of detachments to the Rhine frontier or elsewhere, and these detachments could be rapidly shipped across to the Continent.

Another point, these troops of the army of occupation were of high value. Their separation from the mainland gave them a spirit of independence and of *esprit de corps*, while the fact of being a frontier force gave them continual experience, and formed them into a seasoned and hard-fighting body of men. At the close of the second century a historian observed that 'the British legions are not a whit behind the Illyrian for bravery and for killing spirit';[2] they proved their valour and their tenacity in the grim battle

---

[1] During the German War of 1914–8 Richborough again became a port for the transport of troops to the Continent.

[2] Herodian, iii. 7, 2.

at Lyons in 193, where they fought to the death for their governor, Clodius Albinus—and Severus only just prevailed. Two centuries later another historian[1] passes much the same verdict (though in less admiring terms), that the British legions were too self-confident, too high-spirited. They must have been a grim, independent and pugnacious set of soldiers.

Another force needs mention, the British fleet. It may seem odd to us that it was originally based on Boulogne, but it was. Its chief work would be convoying transports and supplies, and co-operation in large expeditions. That it supported Agricola, and that under his instructions it circumnavigated Britain and so proved it to be an island, we know; that detachments of it assisted in the building of Hadrian's Wall—perhaps swearing as only marines can swear—inscriptions tell us; that it co-operated with the land forces in Septimius' campaigns is a reasonable inference from coins. Though we hear little of it otherwise, that is perhaps simply evidence that it was doing its work. In the late third century the usurper Carausius, who knew something about the uses of a fleet, may have initiated a new system of defence, based upon land-forts (on estuaries or with harbours) from which small squadrons of naval units could operate. These ships could give early warning of the approach of the Saxons, and so the garrison horsemen could deal with an expected landing. But,

[1] Zosimus, iv. 35.

whoever began it, Constantius was almost certainly the perfecter of the scheme; in its complete form the Saxon Shore comprised a round dozen of forts[1] from Brancaster to Bradwell, and from Reculver to Porchester and to Carisbrooke in the Isle of Wight, and possibly a post on Alderney[2] linked the British system with the corresponding Gallic forts. On the French side of the Channel we can be certain of stations at Boulogne and Rouen, at Coutances and Avranches, and near St. Malo, but although there are other names their identification is by no means certain.[3] This set of forts and naval depots did provide some security for the English Channel, and something similar was needed to protect Wales and the west coast against the Irish pirates.

A late Roman fort at Caernarvon, down by the waterside (Caer Seiont), and Roman fortifications at Caer Gybi (on Holyhead) suggest that a watch may have been kept there; in the south-west Carmarthen was certainly occupied during the fourth century, and a typical 'Saxon Shore' type of fort exists at Cardiff. On the south side of the Bristol Channel there appear to be two Roman signal-stations at Martinhoe and Old Burrow (to the west and east of Lynton), and these must have been intended to give warning to the inhabitants

---

[1] See map 2 at end of book.
[2] A suggestion due to Mr. T. D. Kendrick.
[3] For these sites see A. Grenier, *Manuel d'arch. gallo-rom.* i, 389 ff. If Constantius was the perfecter of the system the old name of Coutances (*Constantia*) appears to recall his name.

of Roman Somerset—a county thick-set with
villae—and possibly across the Channel to Cardiff.[1]
It must be admitted that so far no signal-stations
have been identified in West Wales, but they may
still exist and await discovery, and there are slight
indications of some inland in the counties of
Montgomery, Radnor, and Brecon.[2]   But there is
at least a probability that the government took
precautions in the west as well as in the east, and
it would be interesting if we could but learn what
was the main base of the scouting-craft (*scafae
exploratoriae*), with camouflaged sails and rigging,
that Vegetius mentions, and where lay the naval
repair depot (*reliquatio*), whose existence is revealed
by an official who made a dedication at Lydney in
Gloucestershire.[3]   Towards the last third of the
fourth century Theodosius initiated a line of
signal-stations, extending from Scarborough up the
Yorkshire coast to Huntcliff; though that is the
most northerly station so far known, there is
strong evidence for other sites on the Durham
coast—by Carr House, Horden, and Ryhope Dene

[1] See R. E. M. Wheeler, *Prehistoric and Roman Wales*, pp. 234–40.
For the North Devon signal-stations see J. P. Bushe-Fox, *Some Notes on
Roman Coast Defences*, *J.R.S.* xxii, 1932, 60 (esp. 71–2).

[2] In the *Royal Commission on Ancient Monuments for Wales, Inventory*,
there are noted two possible sites in Montgomeryshire, No. 287, at *Cefn-y-
Coed*, east of Kerry, and No. 419, *Y Gaer*, on Gibbet Hill, near Llanfair
Caereinion.   In Radnorshire there is No. 536, *The Gaer*, Newchurch, at
a height of 1,171 ft., with a fine view to the south and the massif of the
Black Mountains.   Further to the west the very names of the Brecon
Beacons, of the camp at *Y Pigwn*, and of *Van* Carmarthen are suggestive.

[3] Vegetius, iv. 37 ; for the *reliquatio* see *CIL.* vii. 137, and also R. E. M.
Wheeler, *Excavations at Lydney*, 1932, 102–4.

up to South Shields—so that the plan may have included the whole East Coast from Humber to Tyne.[1] Indeed, our island may actually have sheltered the Roman mainland by drawing upon itself the first fire of raiders. Britain was wealthy and alluring: 'it is an island,' begins Bede, 'rich in fruits and in trees, well fitted for breeding cattle and horses' (Bede, *H. E.* i. 1)—a description which must apply to Britain as the Romans left it, for what happened between 400 and 600 can hardly have helped.

Thus we return to our question: what did Rome now find here that induced her to defend and to cling to Britain so tenaciously. Likely enough, as we have seen (p. 16) up to about 150 the province had not proved useful, apart from its positional value and its manpower; it was then that Appian noticed that 'even the half of the island which the Romans now hold is not profitable to them' (p. 17). After this date, however, the wealth and productivity of Britain mounted steadily. What was that wealth, and how did the Romans benefit by it? Let us look at the various categories, beginning with mineral wealth. I intend no exhaustive catalogue, naturally, for the evidence has been collected and set out admirably in various publications;[2] all that is necessary for our purpose is a general survey.

[1] See *J.R.S.* ii, 1912, 215, and C. T. Trechmann in *Proc. Soc. Antiq. Newcastle*, Ser. 4, x, 1946, No. 10, 341.

[2] As for example, L. C. West, *Roman Britain, the Objects of Trade*, and R. G. Collingwood, in vol. iii of T. Frank's *Economic Survey of the Roman Empire*.

Of gold, whatever may have been the early hopes of some, the Romans found little, and that little mainly in Wales; there is certainly evidence that they mined it at Dolaucothy, in Carmarthenshire, where water was brought some seven miles, by a special channel, from the river Cothy. There is no clear indication that they either knew of, or worked, the resources of Merionethshire. Silver could be obtained from lead by cupellation, but could not otherwise be mined in our island, and of lead there was abundance, such abundance, indeed, that other interests succeeded in getting a law passed restricting the output of British lead.[1] It was worked on the Mendip Hills (and we may note that within six years of the conquest it was being mined there), in the border district to the south-west of Shrewsbury (for example, near Llanymynech), and on Halkin Mountain in Flintshire (here again, working apparently started before the end of the first century). So, too, the lead-field of Derbyshire was known, and was certainly being worked by the reign of Hadrian, while the lead of Western Yorkshire had been discovered before the first century was out. Lastly, it seems likely that the lead-field in the region of Alston, in the South Tyne valley, was exploited, though the indications of date are not so definite. What is worth noting is the early date at which many of these fields were in operation, as e.g. on the Mendips, in Flintshire, and in West Yorkshire,

[1] Pliny, *N.H.* xxxiv. 49.

and also that British lead-ore was of a higher grade than the Spanish and ultimately ousted it. This lead was useful not only in Britain itself, but also on the Continent, and we can infer from finds of lead-ingots that the main harbours for export must have been Chester, Brough-on-Humber (about six miles west of Hull), and the south country ports.

Tin was found (as far as I know) only in Cornwall, and although in the Flavian period some Roman settlers worked tin there for about fifty years, probably they could not profitably compete with the Spanish tin, and the settlement closed down. But by the middle of the third century, if not earlier, came a change: Spanish tin was exhausted, and once again Cornish supplies became of importance. Roman coins now appear in Cornwall, and the occurrence of mile-stones suggests that short lengths of road were constructed, perhaps from the mines to the nearest convenient ports for shipping. Here the mines must have been worked by native labour, though supervised and directed by imperial officials. Up to the present, however, no direct road-connection between Western Cornwall and the rest of England has been discovered, and transport appears to have been by sea.

Iron ore exists in such quantities under our soil that it is not surprising that the Romans were able to exploit it: their main sources seem to have been the Weald and the Forest of Dean; besides these, traces of iron-working and of iron-smelting appear in Glamorgan, in Herefordshire, and in the East Midlands. On the other hand copper was apparently obtained almost entirely from Welsh sources, principally from Llanymynech—I am aware that this village is technically in England, but for the moment I am annexing it for Wales—from mines on the Great Orme's Head, and (almost certainly) from Parys Mountain in Anglesey.

So much for minerals, and even this summary statement should be enough (I trust) to demonstrate that Britain could make a material contribution to the Empire's wealth. The resources in capital and labour available in Roman hands made exploitation possible on a scale never attempted before; iron, lead, and copper could all be useful for the imperial armies, tin and lead were certainly exported to the Continent, and could be combined to make pewter for local uses. So, in the fourth century British pewter makes its appearance in houses and estates; only the rich could afford dinner-services of silver-plate, but pewter dishes and goblets could decorate more modest tables. Another example of what could be achieved by the skill and capital available to the Roman government is the use of water mills. In the first century farmers and peasants in Italy were using the water power of their rivers to a considerable extent, and recent exploration on the English Roman wall has revealed the existence on the line of the wall of at

least three 'undershot' water mills;[1] I find it hard
to believe that these were the only examples.
The reservoir at Dolaucothy is still called *Melin y
Milwyr* (Soldiers' Mill); the Welsh word for a mill
is still Melin (from the Latin *molina*). Legend
tells that an Irish king, Cormac mac Airt, sent
to this country for a skilled engineer when he
wanted a water mill constructed.[2] Just as the
Romans exploited more fully our mineral resources
so their engineers were the first to harness our
water power.

Arts and crafts call for some mention, however
brief. Rome undoubtedly taught Britons the art
of building and construction in stone and in wood:
for the first time in its history our island saw great
public (and some private) buildings in stone—
temples, administrative offices, and headquarters,
shops, market-places, inns, and pillared colonnades.
So, from the Romans (as much of the vocabulary
of modern Welsh proves) the 'Brittones' learnt how
to shape and carve stone, and how to build with it,
together with the craft of carpentry. These native
regiments served their apprenticeship under legionaries before removal to Germany in 145–6.[3] Thus
at need the Roman government could draw on
skilled manpower. In the late third century
towns in France had been badly damaged by the

---

[1] Pliny, *N.H.* xviii. 97; I. A. Richmond, *Handbook to the Roman Wall*,
ed. 10, 1947, 80, 147, and 166.

[2] C. E. Stevens, in *Mélanges Radet* (=*Rev. Et. Anc.* xlii, 1940, 671).

[3] See F. Drexel, *Bauten u. Denkmäler der Brittoner an d. Limes*, Germania,
vi, 1922, 31.

barbarian raiders: rebuilding was imperative, labour was scarce, but the Emperor Constantius was equal to the occasion; to rebuild Autun he brought over from Britain stonemasons 'of which those provinces had plenty' ('quibus illae provinciae redundabant')[1]—even if you make allowance for the exuberance of a panegyrist, that phrase is highly revealing.

But there were other arts and crafts of great value to Rome—and perhaps the most important were those connected with agriculture and rural industries. The big farming estates (*villae*) not only carried out general farming, crops, and cattle and sheep, but often added to that fulling or tile-making. Many *villae* were situated in the southern midlands and central southern counties of England, and an imperial weaving establishment (producing clothing, rugs, blankets, etc., for the army) was situated at Winchester.[2] Taken together, this suggests large flocks of sheep, and an interest in sheep-breeding; we know that in other provinces, e.g. Spain, Romans were interested in improving the breeds of sheep in order to obtain finer wool, and careful examination of archaeological remains might disclose information about the downland sheep and their history. For British cloaks and wraps were certainly well known. Much the same applies to cattle: as ox-hides could be used by the army not only for boots and shoes, but for

[1] *Paneg. Lat.* (ed. W. Baehrens, 1911) viii. 21 (247).
[2] *Not. Dign. Occ.* xi. 60.

tents—(army tents were made of flaps of leather, and *not* of canvas; hence the army slang term for them, *papiliones*, 'butterflies')—and also for shields, the Romans had every inducement to encourage cattle-breeding: pig-breeding, too, for that matter, since pigs supplied one of the essential items of a soldier's food, lard and fat (*laridum*). Again, horse-breeding must have proved useful for cavalry, and one matter on which we want more information is whether Rome introduced new breeds of horses into our island. Some forty years ago, the late Dr. James Curle produced an account of his excavations at Newstead, on the river Tweed, which was a model of what archaeological publication should be, and included a careful examination of the animal remains.[1] It was evident that in that Roman camp at Newstead there were native ponies, as we might expect, but also a number of better bred horses, measuring about 14 hands, belonging to the cavalrymen and almost certainly brought in from France; finally some large and more powerful big-headed animals belonged probably to the native German breeds, about which Caesar speaks so slightingly, calling them 'bad and ugly.'[2] It seems unlikely that the better bred horses left no trace in post-Roman Britain, the more so when we recollect that the Celts had such a variety of chariots, traps, gigs, and other horse-drawn vehicles

[1] J. Curle, *A Roman Frontier-Post . . .*, Glasgow, 1911, esp. 362–71. At Caerwent animal remains revealed two kinds of horses: *Bull. Board Celt. Stud.* v, 1929–31, 390.

[2] Caesar, *de Bell. Gall.* iv, 2, 2 'praua atque deformia.' Some MSS. read, however, *parua* for *praua*.

that the Romans took the Celtic names over into their own language,[1] and when we remember, too, the Celtic love of horses. One of the most vigorous and exciting representations of a chariot-race that I know is given on a tessellated pavement found at Horkstow in Lincolnshire (p. 20, n. 1), and in Lincoln city the keen eye of Dr. I. A. Richmond recovered a fine piece of sculpture showing a young charioteer intent on his driving. I feel no doubt that the Roman occupation marks a definite stage in British horse-breeding.

Many other matters might be mentioned, but I must concentrate on one only—corn growing. Under the Empire the native farmers and workers carried on their patient toil, but the fields became larger, and at least one district, the Fenland, shows signs of extensive cultivation; it may well have been a large imperial corn estate, with its administrative centre probably at Castor (near Stamford).[2] The production of grain was of the first importance for the armies, and we may judge how successful and plentiful corn-production had become from the fact that not only was it sufficient for the needs of the island, but also provided for the troops stationed in Germany: in fact, on one occasion, in 359, when Julian was making an inspection of the devastated Rhineland areas, where the battered cities had not enough food either for themselves or

---

[1] Nearly a dozen; see A. Holder, *Alt-keltischer Sprachschatz*, 1897, for such words.

[2] The suggestion is that of Prof. C. F. C. Hawkes.

E

for the hundreds of returned prisoners-of-war, the prince made the provincials build a fleet of 800 transport vessels, and ferry over from Britain sufficient grain to meet the emergency.[1]

I have now described briefly what seem to me the main military and economic advantages accruing to the Roman Empire from the occupation of our country. I might add that the recurring possibility of raids and of frontier-skirmishes must have made it a most useful training-ground for recruits and for testing new tactics. North of Haltwhistle, and by Cawthorn in Yorkshire, can still be discerned (as could be once on Llandrindod Common), traces of practice camps, where recruits were put through training in digging and entrenching. As to tactics, one governor was actually executed by the suspicious Emperor Domitian, because he had invented a new type of cavalry lance, and called it by his own name. But I do not wish to suggest that governors spent their whole time fighting; far from it—there was justice to be cared for, and a hundred-and-one details of administration. The governor would be responsible for justice, for law and order; in his province were various types of towns and communities, colonies such as Colchester, Lincoln, Gloucester, and York; cantonal capitals of tribes, such as Silchester or Caerwent or Wroxeter, where a local senate conducted administration; smaller villages and settlements. Outside what we may call 'the

[1] Julian, 279D and 280C : Ammian, xviii. 2, 3 ; Zosimus, iii. 5, 2.

Civil Zone' many tribes must still have remained under the leadership and control of their chieftains; in the earliest days a king of the Regnenses, by name Tib. Claudius Cogidubnus, had been at once king of his tribe and an official of the emperor, and the local princes and chieftains must often have stood in close relations to the imperial governor, who might recognize their service and loyalty with gifts, or the grant of citizenship, or with honours and insignia.[1]

In all his multifarious tasks the governor could draw on the experience both of Roman officers and of industrious provincials; a letter from one governor, Tib. Claudius Paulinus, that is still extant,[2] suggests that even governorship had its compensations, and that governors could afford to reward honest service generously. Tib. Claudius Paulinus was governor of Lower Britain in 220. While he was at York, he had among his court assessors a provincial from Gaul, by name Sennius Sollemnis. Paulinus rated his service so highly, that he not only paid his stipend in gold, but added some presents, and Sollemnis was so proud of the letter which accompanied them that he had it preserved on stone.

'Though you deserve more,' writes Paulinus, 'yet I hope you will be pleased to accept these few gifts, since they are offered to you in compliment:

---

[1] For Cogidubnus see *CIL*. vii, 11 ; see pp. 27–8 for the significance of the Latin names of Cunedda's ancestors, and for a hypothesis about the recognition and reward of one of them, Patern (*Paternus*) by Magnus Maximus.
[2] *CIL*. xiii. 3162.

A wrap of Canusine wool, an embroidered Laodicean dalmatic, a gold brooch with gems, two thick rugs, a British *tossia*,[1] and a seal-skin. I will send you the official recognition of your six-monthly service as soon as, shortly, I have a little more time. Pray accept the salary due for that period of service in gold, with the approval of the gods and of his sacred majesty the Emperor; in future you will receive for such deserts gifts more worthy of my feelings towards you.'

This has been only an outline, and much I have perforce omitted. I had no intention of describing and detailing the economic life of the island—the local potteries, the carving of articles from jet or shale or 'Blue John,' the commerce across the Channel to the Rhineland provinces or to France, the export of hounds, the traffic in slaves between barbarian lands and Roman, with all the vicissitudes of fortune that war produces[2]—such topics will be found amply treated in other books. But I have tried in the preceding pages to indicate briefly something of the value that Britain possessed for the Roman Empire. Raiders made it their target because here was something worth raiding, cattle and sheep, cloth and hides, silver and lead and iron, a wealthy material civilization. The Roman occupation had developed Britain into a rich and

---

[1] A *tossia* is interpreted as some kind of wrap or rug. It is worth noting how much of the present consists of warm clothing or wraps.

[2] As, for example, the adventures of a slave-woman as revealed by *Digest* xlix. 15, 6, and interpreted by E. B. Birley in *M. Cocceius Firmus* (see bibliography).

flourishing island; raiders might carry off some of these riches, they could loot silver-plate, might burn and ravage buildings, but they could not destroy its sources. 'Fortunate Britain,' cries a panegyrist,[1] 'more blessed now than all other lands . . . Rightly has nature lavished on you all the blessings of climate and soil, where neither the hardness of winter nor the heat of the summer is too great, where there is such fertility of crops as suffices for the gifts both of Ceres and of Bacchus' —(he means bread and beer)—'Where there are forests but no giant beasts' (as in Northern Europe) 'where there are lands but no poisonous creeping things, but rather an incalculable number of flocks and herds full of milk and laden with fleeces . . .' Grave, indeed, reflects another,[2] would the loss of such a land as Britain be to the Empire, 'a land with such a wealth of fruits, rejoicing in so great a number of pastures, abounding with veins of ore in so many mines, so profitable in its revenues, girt with so many harbours, so vast in its circuit.' Still, the sober-minded may reflect, it is the business of a panegyrist to be—panegyrical. Granted that, we may yet note that when a Gallic writer, Constantius, is recounting the life of St. Germanus and relates the saint's two visits here, he regards Britain as being 'first or largest of all the islands there are,' and speaks of it as 'a most wealthy island' (*opulentissima insula*).[3] Less than three

---

[1] *Pan. Lat.* (ed. W. Baehrens) vi. (vii), 9, 207.
[2] Ibid. viii (v), 11, 239.
[3] Constantius, *Vita S. Germani* (ed. W. Levison), 18.

centuries elapse and Bede, in that noble opening to his *Ecclesiastical History*, exalts the wealth of our country in crops and trees, its fitness for breeding flocks and herds and horses, its birds, its fishes, its seals, its hot springs, its mines.

Britain was indeed a wealthy island; it had become so during the course of those three and a half centuries since Claudius first landed; that was one of the reasons why the Romans clung to it. Some of the most experienced and wisest heads among the emperors—Vespasian, Hadrian, Severus, Aurelian, Diocletian, men not prone to act from motives of sentiment or of mere prestige—had decided to retain it; they had hard heads, they were good judges. Our Saxon forefathers, also, knew what they wanted—a land to be desired, a land to settle in; their early graves show, too, that they could find plenty of employment for the craftsmen and jewellers and artificers among the British population. And I fancy that the sentence in the *Anglo-Saxon Chronicle* recording how the Romans had so buried their treasures that no man could find them[1] reflects a certain chagrin on the part of disappointed treasure-seekers.

This is, you may think, too rosy a view. At the end many of the towns were shrunken, some almost derelict, and their population reduced to a low cultural level.[2] But I have been speaking mainly

---

[1] See above, pp. 35–6.

[2] But a note of caution should be sounded here, as my friend Dr. Richmond reminded me; comparatively few towns have been sufficiently thoroughly excavated for us to pronounce a verdict confidently.

of the country, and of its resources, and there the picture is far more favourable; exaggeration there may be in the panegyrists, an element of patriotic pride in Bede, but Constantius had no motive for exaggeration. Still, lest you should think this account too favourable, I have reserved for the close one gloomy topic, the use of Britain as a place of exile or a penal island. For this there is certainly evidence: Marcus Aurelius sent a high-spirited Armenian prince to end his days in banishment here;[1] a turbulent Pannonian, exiled to Britain, lost his life in an endeavour to stir up his fellow-prisoners to revolt and escape;[2] when Magnus Maximus was condemning the Priscil-lianist heretics—a deed which moved the good St. Martin to anger against the malevolent bishops who had counselled him—he deported two, Instan-tius and Tiberianus, 'to the isle of Sylinancis, which lies beyond Britain' (*In Sylinancim insulam, quae ultra Britannias sita est*).[3] Sylinancis is usually taken to mean the Scilly Isles, which the French still term *Sorlingues*. Far away, beyond the limits of the civilized world, on storm-beaten rocks, these condemned men were to purge their heresy.

One last task remains: to estimate what *we* have derived from the Romans; to that fascinating topic I propose to devote my final lecture.

[1] Dio Cassius, lxxi. 14, 2.
[2] Ammian, xxviii. 3, 4.
[3] Sulpicius Severus, *Chron.* ii. 51.

IV

WHAT WE HAVE GAINED FROM THE ROMAN OCCUPATION

IF we ask ourselves what we owe to the Roman occupation one fact stands out clearly. For the first time in its history our country emerges as a whole, one unified territory, organized and governed from a centre, intended to function as a unit, 'the Britains.' The man finally responsible (under the emperor) for the safety and integrity of this territory was the military commander, earlier termed a *Legatus*, and later 'the Duke of the Britains' (*Dux Britanniarum*). That title, as we shall see, lived long in men's memory, as did the fact of one united territory, the bond of union being a common loyalty towards the 'eternal' emperor and the name of the 'eternal city,' Rome.

This unity was at once manifested in and strengthened by language, communications, culture, art, and religion, and at the present day we are still being influenced by them, in so far as they are the bone and marrow of our modern culture. That is what we have inherited from the Roman occupation of Britain, however much some earlier historians failed (or refused) to recognize it. Let us look at these factors severally.

1. LANGUAGE. So strong was the impress of the Roman language, and of Roman civilization, that even where Romans did not conquer they yet left their mark on that periphery. This can be

observed in both old Irish and old German. There was never a Roman conquest of Ireland, and such trading contacts as took place seem to have been principally with the north-east and the south-east;[1] yet in old Irish certain words derive directly from the Latin language talked by the traders who touched the Irish shores. Thus the words for some weights and measures descend from the Latin *uncia, sextarius, modius;* for currency from *denarius, moneta,* and for some articles of luxury from *aurum, vinum, purpura.* Significantly, too, our Teutonic ancestors took over and handed down to us two words for important operations, buying and selling, which came from their meeting with Roman slave-dealers, and Roman inn-keepers; *mango,* 'a slave-dealer,' and *caupo,* 'an inn-keeper' or 'huckster,' have survived to our time in those words which end in -*monger* ('ironmonger,' 'cheese-monger,' 'warmongering') or contain the element -*cheap* or -*cheaping*—Cheapside, or Chipping Campden, or Chipping Norton, or 'cheapjack.'[2]

If this is true of unconquered territories much deeper was the influence in this country of Latin, which for nearly four hundred years was the official language, spoken in law-courts and at public ceremonies, learnt by recruits at drill and brought back by them in their retirement, taught at the schools, and used generally as the language of intercourse. Rome brought new things and

---

[1] See S. O'Riordain's article in the bibliography.
[2] See T. Kleberg, *Mango,* in *Eranos* xliii, 1945, 277.

new arts to this country, and together with them she imposed on our Celtic ancestors (and on their language, old British) new names for those things. Those names have often survived into a language still spoken here, into modern Welsh; let me merely remark summarily here that many Welsh terms still in use for shipping—anchor, oar, port, ship; or for building—wall, partition-wall, door-post, gate, transom, window, step; for country work—pitchfork, bridle, halter, saddle, manger, mill and well; and for such civilized things as inns and shops, for instruments used in eating and drinking, and writing; for vegetables and fruits and trees, and for that highly civilized thing, washing[1]—many of these terms still in everyday use, derive from the Latin language, and from what the Romans taught our ancestors. To some of these topics I shall return later, but the general significance may be stated briefly and dogmatically now. These new words for new things came over into Celtic, and have survived to this day as a lasting heritage—and I must here acknowledge and pay my debt of gratitude to the writings and to the personal kindness of Professor Henry Lewis, of Mr. Thomas Jones, and of Professor Kenneth Jackson for making me better acquainted with the importance of them.

One caution must be interposed: in a large number of 'technical terms' Welsh derived directly

---

[1] Welsh 'sebon,' *soap* and 'ysbwng,' *sponge*, derive direct from Latin.

from Latin. But we must not assume that Latin was spoken everywhere. In towns and cities there is some evidence for its diffusion among all classes; potters sign their names in Latin, workmen reckon their tallies or inscribe sarcastic messages, or make up itemized lists . . . these are convincing. But just as in the provinces of Gaul the native Gallic continued to be spoken in mountain glens and distant country—which explains why Irenaeus taught himself Gallic, in order better to preach the word[1]—so British-Celtic continued to be spoken commonly in the south-west, in Wales, and in the north-west. Doubtless the farmers and others who went to the towns would know what I may term 'market-Latin,' the names for the produce they brought—hams, or vegetables, or eggs, or cloth, or fruit—they would know how to reckon in Latin numerals, but that was all. At home, on the farm, or in their villages, they would speak Celtic. With this caution it is fair to remark that Welsh has a strong basic element of Latin.[2]

2. COMMUNICATIONS. This was a factor of great power in unification: nothing like it had been experienced before. The Romans did not invent roads, but they certainly made peculiarly their own the art of constructing highways, properly levelled and aligned, with deep foundations and fine paving, and with ditches to carry off surplus water.

---

[1] Irenaeus, *contra Haereses* i, *praef.* 3.

[2] An authoritative and convincing analysis and explanation of British Vulgar Latin has now been given by Professor K. H. Jackson; see his article cited in the Bibliography.

Originally, in a conquered territory, the roads they built were designed to connect headquarters and the forts together; along these supplies could be brought up, and infantry could march (or cavalry ride) securely to their stations. But in time the system developed to such an extent that a network of roads covered the whole country, and opened up districts to exploitation and to commerce as well. There is no need to describe the great trunk roads, and the many lateral ones; the scope and comprehensiveness of the road-system laid down by the Romans is best exemplified by the fact that many of our main roads are still built upon Roman foundations, or follow the same lines: where there are divergencies the Industrial Revolution has been accountable, or local history, or lack of resources, e.g. where near Lichfield the Watling Street swings inconveniently through two right-angled turns, because a straight course would cross marshy ground. The Romans drove the roadway across that marsh on piles of alder wood; later ages could not.

But the Roman strategists arranged that wherever possible their important bases should be accessible not only by land but by sea, too. York, Newcastle, Chester, Caernarvon, Carmarthen, Cardiff, and Caerleon are sufficient proof. In Wales the road and communications system were far more logically planned in Roman days than in later centuries. Even in the palmiest times of the Railway Age I doubt whether a man could have travelled much quicker from Caernarvon to Cardiff than he could have gone on horseback along Sarn Helen from the north to the forts at Carmarthen or Brecon. Which prompts me to utter the hope that steady investigation will be made during the coming years of the course of these roads through central Wales; the Ordnance Survey *Map of Roman Britain*, with commendable caution, marks only those sections of roads of which it is absolutely certain, and so leaves several forts marooned. But they must have been linked with each other; what is badly needed is some team-work by eager investigators. And I fancy that search through early documents, such as Lives of the Saints might well produce evidence for the later use of them.

In connection with communications we may notice how well Rome grasped the natural sites for cities, and how her choice has been approved by history. In proof—London, Bath, Chichester, Lincoln, Colchester, Exeter, Chester, York, New-castle, Carlisle, Worcester, Winchester are still surviving either as big cities, or as important centres. By contrast we may note that Silchester and Caister-by-Norwich, which were tribal capitals, failed to endure, and we may ask ourselves why. In the central western section we still have respect-ably sized towns at Chester, Caernarvon, Carmarthen, Neath, and Cardiff, but Caerleon has had to yield to the newer port (Newport), and Caerwent remains a village. Yet all in all we may fairly claim that the essentials of a communications system for Britain, and the sites of most of the great towns were long ago seized and chosen by the Romans; within certain limits the Romans produced urbanization on the right sites and at the right centres.[1] We may compare the work that they did in England and Wales with the effect that the Norman conquest of Ireland had upon that country, where their foundation of towns 'was the most fruitful thing the Normans ever did. They began civic life in Ireland.'[2]

For a third topic I choose the slightly vague term Culture. Here let us begin with the soil, and take agriculture and horticulture as our theme. Before Caesar's time, the Belgae from across the Channel, with their wheeled ploughs, had begun the assault on the heavier soils of our land; slowly, agriculture moved off the uplands down into the valleys. The great financial resources of the Romans enabled them to develop this work, and it now appears almost certain that the Fenland—from Peterborough to King's Lynn —had become, by the third century, imperial domain land devoted to the production of corn, with an administrative centre possibly at Castor (p. 57). Air photography has revealed under our present field layout a complete system of smaller fields and farms, and it must have been from this

[1] C. E. Stevens, *E.H.R.* lii, 1937, 193.
[2] S. O'Faolain, *The Irish*, 1948, 55–6; see also 31 for a contrast with Roman Britain.

region that the Emperor Julian was able to relieve a famine in the Rhineland cities by diverting British corn in a specially-built fleet (pp. 57–58). All over Britain evidence, whether it be the statuette of the ploughman and his oxen coming from Durham, or the remains of farmsteads in Yorkshire, or the big rural industrial estates in the Cotswolds (as at Chedworth), accumulates to show how real was the prosperity and productive power of the farmers and landowners in the third century, and although some coastal districts—notably South Wales and Eastern Anglia—suffered from raiders, inland that prosperity continued unimpaired.

But the Romans were not so devastatingly hard-headed as they are often represented to be, and one taste they shared in common with us was gardens and flowers. Even in the town houses space was left for a flower garden, and we may well remind ourselves of what a debt we owe to the Romans for flowers, vegetables, fruits, and trees. That debt is not always realized, yet the evidence of language (as well as of archaeological remains) seems to me strong: a comparison of names and terms in such languages as French, Welsh, Flemish, and German suggests (to my mind) that the Romans brought in and transplanted to this northern island a great variety of trees, fruits, vegetables, and flowers. Among flowers we can safely include roses, violets, poppies, lilies, and pansies, and it cannot be mere chance that in Welsh, Flemish, and French the words for such

71

delicious things as cherries, medlars, sweet chest-
nuts, and vines all go back to common origin in
Latin. I know that some scholars hold that most
of these fruits are introductions of the Middle Ages,
but to me the linguistic evidence seems overwhelming, quite apart from the fact that early in
the ninth century Charlemagne was already order-
ing the planting of more trees of this type in his
domains.[1]

I think that it is extremely likely that a number
of our fruit-trees—some varieties of apples, grapes,
and cherries—were originally introduced here by
the Romans. Of the cherry we can be quite
certain, for we know its history;[2] of vines, of some
other fruits, and of some nuts, reasonably certain.[3]
Thus, at Langton in East Yorkshire, the excavators
discovered in a Roman well twigs and shells of
walnut, together with twigs of the sweet chestnut
and of the cherry.[4] Such a discovery, linked with
what we know already about Romano-British
flora from Silchester and Caerwent, suggests considerable importation or transplantation of trees
under Roman government.[5]

The same might be said of some of our vegetables

---

[1] Capitularia reg. Franc. ed. A. Boretius, 1881, 90 (= *Mon. Germ. Hist.*
Legum Sectio II, Tomus I).

[2] Pliny, *N.H.* xv, 102 says explicitly that the cherry had been introduced
into Britain.

[3] For vines and viticulture in Britain see S.H.A. *Probus*, 18, 8.

[4] P. Corder and J. L. Kirk, *A Roman Villa at Langton* . . ., 1932, 55.

[5] Mr. A. H. Hoare (see bibliography) considers that cherries, some varieties
of apple, and plums and damsons, were introduced by the Romans, while
the sloe and bullace are indigenous.

—cabbages,[1] broad beans, and so on; and of some trees and shrubs—such as box, plane, and laurel.[2] Here, for the moment, we must rely mainly on linguistic evidence, but botanists and archaeologists can both help to throw light. Let no one think these topics trivial: if these contentions about fruits, flowers, vegetables, and trees are well-founded, we not only owe an aesthetic and sentimental debt to the Romans for the beauty of our countryside, but we also possess data of importance to students of sociology for the diet of our ancestors.

If, however, culture is to be understood in a wider sense let us consider reading and letters, and the arts of organized civilization. In an earlier lecture I spoke about the schools established by the Romans; by the fourth and fifth centuries our island was educating men who could write and preach effectively. It is something that we produced a really notable heretic, Pelagius, whose writings and discourses were known to be dangerously persuasive, just because their Latin was good and clear. St. Patrick is only a little junior to him, an evangelist after a heretic, and though he protests his 'rusticitas' (that is his lack of polish and urbanity), the famous Confession, so clear, so forthright, so simple and sincere, is a monument to British faith and learning. For St. Patrick was steeped in the Bible—not the first Briton to whom

[1] Dr. I. A. Richmond tells me from information supplied by Mr. E. B. Birley that in a well at the H.Q. at Chesterholm, of Theodosian date, was discovered a cabbage-stalk.
[2] For the plane in North Gaul, see Pliny, N.H. xii, 6.

F

that book proved an inspiration—and can be at turns humble or forceful, pleading with or rebuking his countrymen. Perhaps a hundred years later comes the learned Gildas, who not only knows the scriptures through and through, but Virgil and other classical authors as well; who still thinks of Latin as our language ('*nostra lingua.*')[1] A late legend has it that St. Cadoc, returning from Ireland, retires with his companions to Brycheiniog, since he learnt that a famous rhetorician named Bachan had recently arrived there '*from Italia.*' When Cadoc heard the report of his learning 'he was seized by a strong desire to be taught Latinity by him in the Roman fasion,'[2] and so placed himself under Bachan's instruction. Latin still lingered on; so immense was its prestige as the language at once of religion and of civilization, that public documents or public monuments must be in Latin; one curious instance of that is the number of tombstones in our country dating from the sixth century and later, where the inscription is in Latin (of a sort), commemorating king or chieftain, or some leader who calls himself PROTICTOR, or TRIBUNUS, or EMERITUS. These titles all once had official significance; by these titles, by the use of Latin, the bearers claim the prestige of something Roman.

Other arts there were, the construction of houses or sheds in stone or wood, the erection of walls and

---

[1] Gildas, 23 ; a point that I first heard from Sir H. I. Bell.

[2] 'Ab illo Romano more Latinitate doceri non minimum optavit.' A. W. Wade-Evans, *Lives of the Celtic Saints : Vita S. Cadoci*, 11 and 12.

fortifications, the building of bridges or of mills. It is no accident that the Welsh words for wall, door-post and window, partition-wall, transom, chair, etc., are all of Latin origin; the memory of imposing buildings reappears in the account of Vortigern's great palace in Caernarvon (Nennius, 40), or of the glittering castle that the Emperor Maxen saw in his dream (in the *Mabinogion*). It is no accident that when later tribes wished to erect barriers they piled up something that looked like a Roman frontier-line, with a ditch in front and a great mound behind. Whether in North Ireland ('The Black Pig's Dyke'), or in East Anglia, or in Wales itself ('Offa's Dyke') the technique is much the same. Foreign kings could rely upon the occasional deserter to teach their people to drill, dig and fight in the Roman manner; did not the Romans leave behind them (in Gildas' elaborate phrase) 'exemplaria instituendorum armorum?' (p. 28).

In quite another walk of life, in the art of cookery and equipment of a kitchen, I fancy the Romans taught much to our ancestors: Tacitus records how that great governor, Agricola, encouraged the Britons to adopt *delenimenta vitiorum*, including elegant dinner parties (*Agric.* 21). In Frankish and Flemish the words for kettle, beaker, knife, cup, flask, and pot (not to mention many others) are all derived from Latin, and since in Welsh too the words for kitchen (*cegin*) and cooking (*cog, cogino*), for platter (*dysgl*) and knife (*cyllell*) and

75

pan (*padell*) and cake (*torth*) and oven (*ffwrn*) all descend directly from Latin, there is some foundation for claiming that here too Rome brought to the Britons a new standard of civilization.

On one other topic, animals, I must touch, however briefly. Just as Romans were concerned with the transplantation of fruit-trees and flowers, so they were with the rearing and breeding of sheep and horses. It would be temerarious to claim that the Romans did not make a great difference in the breeding of horses and sheep in a land which (as the venerable Bede realized) is eminently well adapted to such purposes. Long after they had departed cavalry played an important part in the military history of Britain, as we know from the traditions about Arthur and his battles, and from the story of the gallant horsemen who rode to their doom at Catraeth (Catterick). On all these topics much still waits to be done by workers in different fields, but done it must be if we are to possess a proper, detailed, and complete picture of the way in which Rome affected the life of these islands.

Of Art itself this is no place to speak at length (and without illustrations). In earlier days there was some talk of Roman classical tradition swamping the Celtic spirit. Nowadays we have enough examples to show that the Celtic artist could go to school with classical antiquity and learn a fineness of technique without losing his originality. When the sky grew darker, British scholars, artists, and craftsmen fleeing for refuge from the invaders to Ireland in the west, helped not only to reinforce the Christian faith, but also to teach the Irish the arts of writing and of illuminating manuscripts; the Irish patterns of decoration are their versions of the classical *motifs*.[1]

Of Religion, again, no long account is needed, because the matter is better known. Christianity was brought to our country under Roman rule and by Roman citizens. Only a few buildings, e.g. at Caerleon and Silchester, have been definitely identified as churches, but there was certainly an early church at Canterbury (Bede, *H.E.*, I, 26) and Cirencester possesses a curious Latin square-word which scholars have recently recognized as Christian.[2] It may well be that remains of other churches lie buried under present-day buildings in those cities which still occupy Roman sites. British bishops took their part in the great assemblies and synods, and a British-born man, St. Patrick, first planted the faith firmly in Ireland, and gained the immortality of becoming a national saint. It looks as though, in that troublous fifth century, rebellious Britons favoured Pelagianism just because it was *not* officially Roman (see p. 36). If only we knew a little more about the circumstances of the time we should understand better both the journey that Victricius

---

[1] See T. C. Lethbridge (loc. cit. 119–26).
[2] See D. Atkinson, *The Sator-Formula* . . . cited in the bibliography. The subject is still controversial ; but see a recent interesting article by J. Carcopino in the bibliography.

of Rouen made to this country (*c.* 395) and
St. Germanus' two visits (pp. 36–38). Even when
pagan invaders had overwhelmed Eastern and
Midland England good work was still being carried
on by British saints in Wales; from Ireland missionaries crossed over into Western Scotland, and
from that region others took Christianity back to
Northumbria. There is a sturdy independence
and individuality about the Christians of the high-
land zone that is very attractive: St. Patrick, St.
Cadoc, St. Illtyd, and the wise Gildas, St. David,
and St. Columba were men full of fire and passion;
they were not easily daunted either by nature or
by man, and could on occasion 'rebuke even kings'
for wrongdoing, as St. Patrick could Coroticus, or
Gildas the rulers of his day.[1]

Much of all this has endured and its influence is
still powerful. Even in the sixth and seventh
centuries there remained both in Wales and
England the memory of a great and powerful
civilization, that could perform feats far beyond the
resources of smaller kingdoms; there lingered the
memory of a great tradition. In the lost province
these post-Romans think of themselves still as
Romani; Cunedda gave to most of his sons 'Roman'
names; everywhere we can discern peoples and
tribes doing what they can to claim a legal right
to rule, conserving Roman tradition and *nostra
lingua,* representing themselves as the constitu-
tional heirs of Rome. The very standard under

[1] I owe this point to my friend Mr. W. O. Chadwick.

which some of them fought, the Red Dragon, was the old imperial ensign,[1] and I would remind you of what one of the greatest Welsh scholars has written of the Gododdin war-band: 'They ride down the Roman road on their white horses, joking and laughing, so the poet says. Clad in heavy Roman armour, fighting from horseback in the Roman way, with javelins, heavy spears, swords, they were not afraid to tackle much superior forces of Saxon infantry.'[2] When Irish writers speak of the country of the Romans they mean—not, as we should imagine, Italy—but Britain, for it had been a united Roman land under one Roman ruler. That ruler had been the *Dux Britanniarum;* the native British kings desire to be *Prydein Wledig*, and when Saxon kings wish to claim legitimacy they transliterate that title as *Bretwald.* Always there is evident the same intent, to claim overlordship over the whole island as the Romans once had done. During those later centuries peoples and tribes could still see about them the remains, imposing even in decay, of walls and gates, of bridges and buildings, and they marvelled at the power that had wrought them. In the seventh century a reeve at Carlisle showed to St. Cuthbert and other visitors the city wall and a fountain in the city itself 'wonderfully built long ago by the Romans'; when the Saxons began to issue coins they could think of no better

---

[1] The Red Dragon : Ammian, xvi. 12, 39.
[2] (Sir) Ifor Williams, *Lectures on Early Welsh Poetry*, 1944, 70.

device than the Roman eagle or the famous
Roman twins.[1]   Gerald of Wales passing by Caerleon remarks on the many vestiges of its former
splendour that may still be seen, of vast palaces
and splendid buildings 'in imitation of the mag-
nificence of Rome' (*Itinerary*, *c*. 5).   These were
achievements far beyond the resources of the small
states and kingdoms of the Dark Ages: Saxons
imagined them to be 'the old work of giants'
('*eald enta geweorc*'), while the Welsh ascribed the
Roman roads through Wales to the legendary
Queen Elen, just as the northern French called
their Roman roads 'chaussées de Brunhaut.'
Indeed, such power and might were evidenced by
these works that later inhabitants could think of
no better author for them than the devil.

I have been speaking of the things that remained
from the Roman occupation, and that still form
part of our material and spiritual heritage from
them. But remember what was lost. Two matters
only I will mention here. Let me remind you,
first, in Sir Cyril Fox's phrasing, how it has always
been 'the tragedy of Britain' that invasions tend
to converge on an area (the south-east) where the
connection with the European mainland is most
quickly cut; when the Romans departed, and
Britain began to be overrun by invaders and
settlers she was cut off from contact with the
countries where some civilization, however impoverished, still existed; nearly two centuries

[1] Vita S. Cuthberti Anon. iv. 8: M. Deanesley in *E.H.R.* lviii, 1943, 129.

80

elapsed before missionaries from Europe landed in Kent. Secondly, the central organization and administration of the whole country broke down; there was no one ruler to study reports and to order repairs when buildings or dykes, or roads, fell into decay. The Cambridgeshire Car Dyke silted up; the cornlands of northern East Anglia slowly become the swampy fenlands of the Middle Ages, and have to wait for ten centuries before drainage begins and they can be rescued again for cultivation; England is parcelled out into a Heptarchy, Wales is divided among quarrelling and rival princes. As for the roads, they crumbled into tracks, still used (I fancy) in medieval campaigns;[1] ten centuries pass and then in 1555, not before, a statute of highways lays upon parishes the duty of keeping up the roads that pass through their territory. That is what was lost: so easy is it to lose grip upon civilized life, so long and so laborious is the road to recovery.

I began these lectures with Commius, the Celtic leader, self-exiled from France, determined to go where he could never see a Roman face more. I end with that last desperate appeal from the Romanized Britons to the great Roman leader in France, Aetius, in or after the year 446, which

---

[1] H. Belloc, *The Road*, 1923, 148, notes that 'much the most of the great battles took place on or near the Roman roads until the twelfth century.' For the importance of Roman roads in campaigns and battles of the seventh century see P. Hunter Blair in *Arch. Ael.* xxvi, 1948, esp. 117–22. For the lack of good road-making in the Middle Ages see L. F. Salzman, *English Trade in the Middle Ages*, 1931, 185–88, esp. 186; 'after the departure of the Roman legions scientific road-making disappeared.'

Gildas records;[1] 'the barbarians drive us back to the sea, the sea drives us back on the barbarians. We can only choose between two kinds of death, to be slaughtered or to be drowned.' It was a last appeal to that power that stood for law and order, civilization, and peace. It might be almost a parable of the curious role that history has commanded our island to play. Geographically Britain is a part of Europe, yet sundered from it by a narrow strait, that has been at different times her salvation and a grave hindrance. In early days our island had been a refuge to peoples flying hither from tyranny or enmity on the Continent, broken men, looking back half in hatred, half in admiration, at the mainland they had left. From that mainland we derive, ultimately, most of the things that have made our life and culture, however much we have moulded them and fashioned them to something of which we may rightly boast, and the Roman occupation was the first, and certainly not the least, of those vital sources, the first achievement of a British unity.

[1] Gildas, 20.

BIBLIOGRAPHY

At the head of this Bibliography I must mention the names of three great scholars who placed the study of Roman Britain on a scientific basis, F. Haverfield, Sir G. Macdonald, and R. G. Collingwood. A bibliography of Haverfield's writings will be found in his posthumous work, *The Roman Occupation of Britain*, Oxford, 1924, pp. 38–57; of Sir G. Macdonald's down to 1931 in *J.R.S.*, XXII, 1932, pp. 3–8, and on to 1940, ibid., XXX, 1940, pp. 129–32; and of R. G. Collingwood's in *Proceedings Brit. Acad.*, XXIX, 1943, pp. 481–85.

I need hardly add that this bibliography does not claim to be complete, but simply to include those writings which have been used by me. An asterisk denotes items that were brought to my notice after the delivery of the lectures in March, 1948.

(1) GENERAL

Atkinson, D.   ..   ..   'Classis Britannica,' *Historical Essays in Honour of James Tait*, Manchester, 1933, pp. 1–11.

Baillie Reynolds, P. K.   ..   'The Roman Occupation of North Wales,' *Trans. Anglesey Ant. Soc. and Field Club*, 1932–33, p. 21.

Birley, E. B.   ..   ..   'Marcus Cocceius Firmus: an epigraphic study,' *Proc. Soc. Ant. Scot.*, LXX, 1935–36, p. 363.

   ..   'Roman Law and Roman Britain,' *Durham Univ. Journal*, March, 1947, p. 58.

   ..   'The Beaumont Inscription, the Notitia Dignitatum, and the Garrison of Hadrian's Wall,' *C. and W. Trans.*, XXXIX, 1939, p. 190.

   ..   'Three Notes on Roman Wales,' *Arch. Camb.*, XCI, 1936, p. 58.

   ..   'Dumfriesshire in Roman Times,' *Trans. Dumfriesshire and Galloway Nat. Hist. and Antiq. Soc.*, XXV, 1947, p. 132.

   ..   *'Britain after Agricola, and the End of the Ninth Legion,' *Durham Univ. Journal*, June, 1948, p. 78.

Bowen, E. G. .. .. *Wales. A Study in Geography and History*, Ed. 2, Cardiff, 1943.
.. 'The Travels of the Celtic Saints,' *Antiq.*, XVIII, 1944, p. 16.
.. 'The Settlements of the Celtic Saints in South Wales,' ibid., XIX, 1945, p. 175.

Breuer, J. .. .. .. *La Belgique romaine*, Brussels, 1944.

Bromwich, R. .. 'The Historical Triads : with special reference to Peniarth MS. 16,' *Bull. Board Celtic Stud.*, XII, 1946 (Nov.), p. 1.

Chadwick, N. K. .. .. 'The Celtic Background of Anglo-Saxon England,' *Yorks. Celtic Studies*, III (*Trans.*, 1940–46), pp. 13–32.

Cheesman, G. L. .. .. *The Auxilia of the Roman Imperial Army*, Oxford, 1914.

Crawford, O. G. S. .. *Topography of Roman Scotland*, Cambridge, 1949.

Curle, J. .. .. .. 'An Inventory of Objects of Roman and Provincial Roman Origin found on Sites in Scotland not definitely associated with Roman Constructions,' *Proc. Soc. Ant. Scot.*, LXVI, 1931–32, pp. 277 ff.

Cumont, Fr. .. .. *Comment la Belgique fut romanisée.* Ed. 2, Brussels, 1919.

Davies, O. .. .. .. *Roman Mines in Europe*, Oxford, 1935.
.. 'Finds at Dolaucothy,' *Arch. Camb.*, XCI, 1936, p. 51.

Deanesley, M. .. .. 'Roman Traditionalist Influence among the Anglo-Saxons,' *E.H.R.*, LVIII, 1943, p. 129.

Forster, M. .. .. *Keltisches Wortgut im Englischen*, Halle, 1921.

Fowler, G. .. .. .. 'Fenland Waterways Past and Present,' *Proc. Camb. Ant. Soc.*, XXXIII, 1933, p. 108, and ibid., XXXIV, 1934, p. 17.

Fox (Sir) Cyril .. *The Personality of Britain*, Ed. 4. Cardiff, 1943.
.. *A Find of the Early Iron Age from Llyn Cerrig Bach, Anglesey.* Cardiff, 1945.

Gresham, C. A. .. .. 'The Roman Fort at Tomen-y-Mur,' *Arch. Camb.*, XCIII, 1938, p. 192.

Hoare, A. H. .. .. *The English Grass Orchard*, 1928 (esp. pp. 18–22).

Hoops, J. .. .. .. *Waldbäume und Kulturpflanzen im germanischen Alterthum*, 1906.

Hunter Blair, P. .. .. 'The Origins of Northumbria,' *Arch. Ael.*, XXV, 1947, p. 1.

Jackson, K. H. .. .. 'On the Vulgar Latin of Roman Britain,' *Medieval Studies in Honor of J. D. M. Ford*, 1948. Cambridge, Mass., pp. 83–103.

Lethbridge, T. C. .. .. 'Merlin's Island,' 1948 ; esp. chapter III, *Roman Britain changes into Saxon England*, pp. 42–77.

Loomis, R. S. .. .. 'From Segontium to Sinadon,' *Speculum*, XXII, 1947, p. 520.

Loth, J. .. .. .. *Les mots latins dans les langues brittoniques*, 1892.

Margary, I. D. .. .. **Roman Ways in the Weald*, 1948.

Marples, M. .. .. *Sarn Helen : A Roman Road in Wales*. Newtown, Mont., 1939.

Miller, S. N. .. .. In *The Roman Occupation of Southwestern Scotland*. Glasgow, 1949, p. 210.

Morris, A. J. .. .. *'The Saxon Shore Fort at Burgh Castle,' *Proc. Suffolk Institute of Archaeology*, 1947, p. 100.

Mortimer Wheeler, R. E. .. 'Segontium and the Roman Occupation of Wales,' *Y Cymmrodor*, XXXIII, 1923, p. 1.

.. 'Roman and Native in Wales : an Imperial Frontier Problem,' ibid., XXXI, 1921, p. 40.

.. *Prehistoric and Roman Wales*. Oxford, 1925.

Nash-Williams, V. E. .. 'Topographical list of Roman Remains found in South Wales,' *Bull. Board Celtic Stud.*, IV., 1928, p. 246.

.. *The Roman Legionary Fortress at Caerleon, Monmouthshire*. Cardiff, 1940.

.. 'Some dated Monuments of the "Dark Ages" in Wales,' *Arch. Camb.*, XCIII, 1938, p. 31.

Nesselhauf, H. .. .. 'Die spätrömische Verwaltung der gallisch-germanischen Länder,' *Abhand. Preuss. Akad*, 1938, Ph.-Hist. Klasse, No. 2. (A shorter and more 'popular' version of this appears in *Forschungen und Fortschritte*, XV, 1939, April 20, p. 155.)

Newstead, R. .. .. 'The Roman Station, Prestatyn,' *Arch. Camb.*, XCIII, 1938, p. 175.

Nicholson, E. W. B. .. 'The Dynasty of Cunedag and the "Harleian Genealogies," ' *Y Cymmrodor*, XXI, 1908, p. 63.

North, F. J. .. .. 'The Map of Wales,' *Arch. Camb.*, XC, 1935, p. 1.

Oswald, F. .. .. .. 'Un indice présumable de la présence de la huitième légion en Angleterre,' *Homenagem a Martins Sarmento, Guimarães*, 1933, p. 269.

Phillips, C. W. .. .. 'The Present State of Archaeology in Lincolnshire,' *Arch. Journal*, XCI, 1934, pp. 110–35.

Pryce, F. N. and Davies, T. (Reports on excavations at Forden Gaer). *Arch. Camb.*, LXXXII, 1927, p. 333; LXXXIV, 1929, p. 100; LXXXV, 1930, p. 115.

Ralegh Radford, C. A. .. 'Roma e l'Arte dei Celti e degli Anglosassoni dal V all' VIII secolo d. C,' *Quaderni dall' Impero*. Rome, 1938.
.. 'The Roman Villa at Low Ham,' *Somerset and Dorset Notes and Queries*, XXV, parts 232 and 235.

Richmond, I. A. .. .. 'The Romans in Redesdale,' *Northumberland County History*, Vol. XV, 1940, pp. 63–154.
.. 'Handbook to the Roman Wall,' Tenth edition. Newcastle-on-Tyne, 1947.
.. *Roman Britain* (Britain in Pictures), 1947.
.. 'Gnaeus Iulius Agricola,' *J.R.S.*, XXXIV, 1944, p. 34.
.. 'The Four Coloniae of Roman Britain,' *Arch. Journal*, CIII, 1946, pp. 56–84.
(And many other articles, notably in the *Antiquaries Journal, Archaeologia, Archaeologia Aeliana*, and *Transactions of the Cumberland and Westmorland Society of Antiquaries*.)

Ó Ríordáin, S. P. .. .. 'Roman Material in Ireland,' *Proc. Roy. Ir. Acad.*, LI, 1947, Section C, No. 3, pp. 35–82.

St. Joseph, K. .. .. 'Air Photography and Archaeology,' *Geogr. Journ.*, CV, 1945, p. 47.

Stenton (Sir) F. M. .. 'The Historical Bearing of Place-Name Studies : England in the Sixth Century,' *Trans. Roy. Hist. Soc.* (Ser. 4), XXI, 1939, p. 1.
.. 'The English Occupation of Southern Britain,' ibid., XXII, 1940, p. 1.

Stevens, C. E. .. .. 'The Civitates of Britain,' *E.H.R.*, LII, 1937, p. 193.
.. 'Gildas Sapiens,' ibid., LVI, 1941, p. 353.
.. 'A possible conflict of laws in Roman Britain,' *J.R.S.*, XXXVII, 1947, p. 132.

Stevens, C. E.	..	..	'The British Sections of the "Notitia Dignitatum,"' *Arch. Journ.*, XCVII, 1940, p. 125.
		..	'Magnus Maximus in British History,' *Etudes Celtiques*, III, Juin, 1938, p. 86.
		..	'L'Irlande et la Bretagne romaine,' *Mélanges Radet* (=*Rev. Et. Anc.*, XLII, 1940), p. 671.
Thompson, J.	..	..	'Ancient Celtic Symptoms in Arthurian Romance,' *Trans. Cymmrodorion* (Session 1936), 1937, p. 137.
Vendryès, J.	..	..	'Le position linguistique du Celtique,' *Proc. Brit. Acad.*, XXIII, 1937.
Williams (Sir) Ifor		..	'The Gododdin Poems,' *Trans. Anglesey Ant. Soc. and Field Club*, 1935, p. 25.
		..	'When did British become Welsh,' ibid., 1939, p. 27.
		..	'The Poems of Llywarch Hên,' *Proc. Brit. Acad.*, XVIII (1934).
		..	*Lectures on Early Welsh Poetry.* Dublin, 1944.

(Accounts in English of Sir Ifor Williams's books on the Gododdin and Llywarch Hên have been published in *Antiquity*, XIII, 1939, pp. 25–34 (K. H. Jackson) and XVI, 1942, pp. 237–57 (C. A. Gresham).)

(2) CHRISTIANITY AND ST. PATRICK

Atkinson, D.	..	..	'The Sator-Formula and the Beginnings of Christianity,' *Bull. John Rylands Lib.*, XXII, No. 2, Oct., 1938.
Bury, J. B.	..	..	*The Life of St. Patrick and his place in History*, 1905.
Carcopino, J.	..	..	'Le Christianisme secret du "carré magique,"' *Museum Helveticum*, V, 1948, fasc. 1, p. 16.
Hazlehurst, R. T. S.		..	*The Works of Fastidius*, 1927.
MacErlean, J.	..	..	'Silva Focluti,' *Analecta Bollandiana*, LVII, 1939, p. 334.
MacNeill, E.	..	..	'The Native Place of St. Patrick,' *Proc. Roy. Ir. Acad.*, XXXVII, 1924–27, p. 118 (publ. 1926).
		..	'Silva Focluti,' ibid., XXXVI, 1921–24, p. 249.
Müller, K. ..	..	..	'Der heilige Patrick,' *Nachr. Wiss. Göttingen*, 1931, Ph.-Hist. Kl., pp. 62–116.
Williams, H.	..	..	*Christianity in Early Britain.* Oxford, 1912.

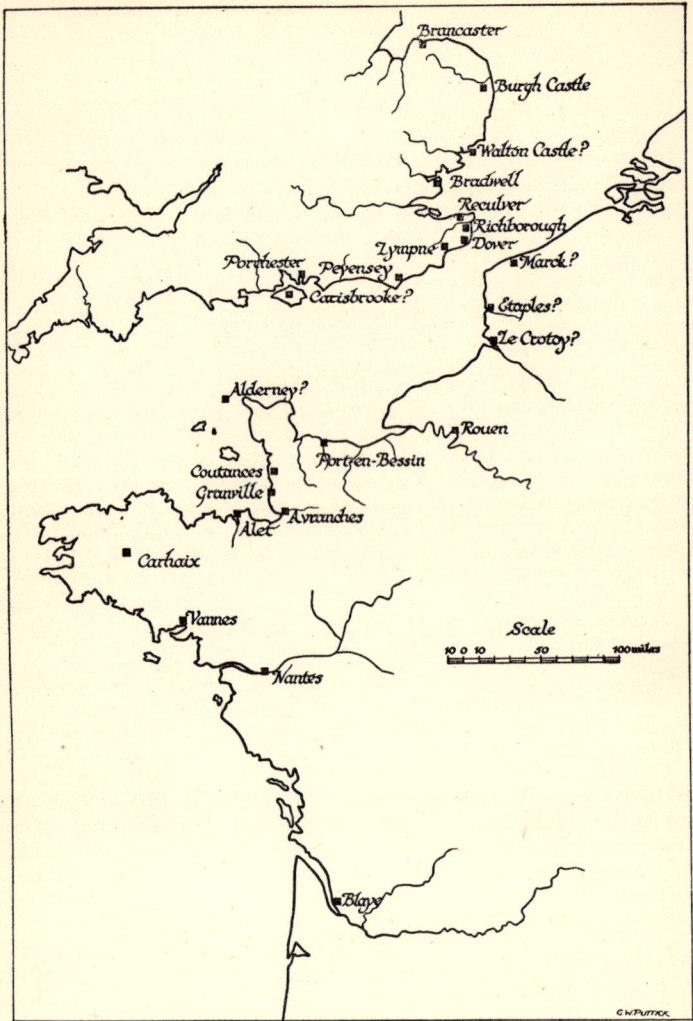

Brancaster
Burgh Castle
Walton Castle?
Bradwell
Reculver
Richborough
Lympne
Dover
Porchester
Pevensey
Marck?
Carisbrooke?
Etaples?
Le Crotoy?
Alderney?
Rouen
Coutances
Portven-Bessin
Granville
Avranches
Alet
Carhaix
Vannes
Scale
10 0 10   50   100 miles
Nantes
Blaye

G.W.PUTTICK

THE SAXON SHORE DEFENCES

88

NOTE UPON MAP 2, THE SAXON SHORE DEFENCES.

The *Notitia Dignitatum* (Oc. XXVIII) furnishes a list of nine forts of the Saxon Shore in Britain—*Othona, Dubris, Lemannis, Branoduno, Garianno, Regulbi, Rutupis, Anderidos, Portum Adurni*. These are mostly identifiable, though there appear to be more surviving (or attested) forts of Saxon Shore type than there are names in the *Notitia*. From north to south these fort-sites are : Brancaster, Burgh Castle (possibly Walton Castle, now submerged), Bradwell-iuxta-mare, Reculver, Richborough, Dover, Lympne, Pevensey, Porchester (and possibly Carisbrooke in the Isle of Wight), making eleven in all.

In France the *Notitia* mentions (Oc. XXXVIII) three sites in Belgica, over the identification of which there has been much controversy : *Marcae* (? near Calais), *Locus Quartensis sive Hornensis* (? mouth of the R. Somme), *Portus Epatiaci* (? Etaples). Further west it records (Oc. XXXVII) ten forts under the command of the *Dux Tractus Armoricani :* I give the ancient names followed by the modern place-names (in brackets) as identified in A. Grenier, *Manuel d'Arch. gallo-rom.* I, 1931, 389–393, who bases himself mainly upon C. Jullian, *Hist. de la Gaule*, VIII, 105–111 ; *Grannona* (? Port-en-Bessin), *Blabia* (Blaye, on the r. bank of the R. Gironde), *Benetis* (Vannes), *Osismis* (Carhaix, in mid-western Britanny), *Manatias* (? Nantes), *Aleto* (Alet, nr. St. Malo), *Constantia* (Coutances), *Rotomago* (Rouen), *Abrincatis* (Avranches), *Grannono* (? Granville).

To these ten forts must be added a possible eleventh on the island of Alderney. Proceeding in a roughly north-to-south direction we get : Rouen, Port-en-Bessin (n. of Bayeux), ? Alderney, Coutances, Granville, Avranches, Alet, Carhaix, Vannes, Nantes, and Blaye. Such a layout raises problems that are varied and difficult, e.g. the connection with the British system, and the apparent neglect of most of the Breton peninsula and its ports. But I have thought it worth while to place all these sites on one map so as to present the picture as a whole, in the hope that it may act (if nothing else) as a starting-point or incentive for further research and investigation. Fruitful advances may well accrue in the future from co-operation between French and English archaeologists in this domain.

M.P.C.

CARDIFF
WILLIAM LEWIS (PRINTERS) LTD.